SMALL BUSINESS: MANAGEMENT AND PERFORMANCE

To Janet, Emma and Sarah

Small Business: Management and Performance

Survival for engineering firms

ALAN HANKINSON

*Faculty of Business, Economics
and Management*
Portsmouth Polytechnic

Avebury

Aldershot · Brookfield USA · Hong Kong · Singapore · Sydney

Published by
Avebury
Academic Publishing Group
Gower House
Croft Road
Aldershot
Hants
GU11 3HR

Gower Publishing Company
Old Post Road
Brookfield
Vermont 05036
USA

A CIP catalogue record for this book is available from the British Library and the US Library of Congress

ISBN 1 85628 032 2

Printed in Great Britain by Billing & Sons Ltd, Worcester

Contents

v

Preface

This 10 year longitudinal study is concerned with small firms' managerial attitudes and performances. It covers a wide range of managerial observations across the spectrum. The findings are intended to provide those interested in the in the small firm sector, i.e. industry itself, local and national government, the consultancy bodies and, not least, the higher education student and lecturer, with a clearer appreciation of the real motivations of, and weaknesses behind, managerial decision making. If used selectively the prospective small firm owner should also find the book of interest and value. With this in mind the material has been presented in a concise descriptive manner and the evidence has to a large extent been allowed to speak for itself. The full story could, of course, occupy several books and might be summarised in a few pages. Any intermediate length provides such difficulties for the writer as to leave him somewhat dissatisfied. Here the usual problems of deciding what to omit and in what way to present the remainder have been intensified by the size of the subject and the multiplicity of its facets. The author's only refuge from his doubts as to whether he has found the best way of achieving what he has attempted is the reflection that the identity of the 'best way' is largely a matter of opinion. In any event the work can only represent an introduction to a subject of immense scope and complexity.

Essentially, the book exposes the problems of small firms, many of which appear to have been self-inflicted. The book does not pretend to offer instant solutions to entrenched small business problems. It does not claim to raise profits overnight. It sets out the problems that small firms should avoid. Problems that some small firms were not even aware they had, but which were revealed during years of consultancy by the writer. The relative performanes of both the small and larger firms, and the mechanical and electrical engineering companies are also highlighted where appropriate. Once these 'barriers within' are understood, only then can meaningful solutions be recommended.

Chapter 1 provides an introduction to the South Wessex Survey. Chapters 2, 3, 4 and 5 cover the investment problem, finance, project appraisal and profitability respectively. Pricing is the subject of Chapter 6. Chapter 7 is concerned with output. Marketing is examined in Chapter 8, whilst Chapter 9 analyses aspects of performance. Chapter 10 offers a summary and a possible approach to the breaking down of the 'barriers within'.

Finally, appreciation is extended to the firms that contributed the data upon which the bulk of the work has been based. All errors and inadequacies are, of course, my own responsibility.

Alan Hankinson
Summer 1991

1 Introduction

Introduction

During the 1960's the U.K. government began to acknowledge that small firms experienced difficulties quite unlike those of larger concerns. The Bolton Committee (1971) was the outset of government awareness of small businesses. The report generated considerable interest at the time of publication. Twenty years on, the work is still widely accepted.

The Bolton Report marked the first major attempt to produce a comprehensive survey of the small firm sector. This area has now been relatively well researched, but even so, the formulation of industrial policy has tended to proceed without a detailed knowledge of the psychology of decision making employed by small business management. Their reaction to government intervention, for example, has been consistently misunderstood.

This is not to say that research has been necessarily inadequate. It has been the interpretation and implementation that might be criticised. Perhaps the most detailed general inquiry prior to the Bolton Report was the

Oxford Survey (1956) undertaken by Bates, Lydall and Stewart. This was presented in a long series of publications. The Midlands Survey (1957) conducted by Jervis was mainly directed at the finance of private companies. Lund and Miner (1971) produced a paper attempting to identify the growth and cyclical performance of small firms using the information provided by the Confederation of British Industry's Industrial Trends Surveys. The survey's results were also used to examine factors such as limitations of output. A particularly interesting study of investment behaviour of small firms was also undertaken by Lund and Miner (1971). The work described the investment behaviour of small firms and compared it with that of larger firms. All this research stimulated some interest in the smaller business. But it was the Bolton Report (1971) and its 18 research reports that catalysed the further research needed throughout the 1970's to the present day. Notwithstanding this flow of work, the Wilson Committee (1979) reporting on the financing of small firms actually made recommendations for a Department of Industry Statistical Unit for the collection of data for small businesses. Whilst theories and surveys of the small firm have been numerous and wide ranging since Bolton, much of the work has, as before Bolton, been of American origin. Unfortunately, whatever the source, very little implementation of the recommendations made by this volume of research occurred. The crystallisation of industrial policy went ahead without a clear grasp of the roles of small firms. The possible impact upon them of the decisions and actions of governments has been equally vague.

Aim of the South Wessex Survey

The intention of this 10 year logitudinal study was to make a specific contribution to the field by examining the motivations of, and the weaknesses behind, investment, pricing, output, marketing, product development, employment creation, training, and information technology decision making in in 50 small firms in the Dorset-Hampshire region. Small firms as suppliers to large organisations, and an appraisal of the managerial effectiveness of the small hotel as a comparison, were also investigated. Throughout the fieldwork a persistent effort was made to ensure that the data collected were representative of how small firms actually did behave as opposed to, or in support of, what the literature over the years had claimed.

2

The small firm sector defined

The Bolton Report (1971) confirmed that the small firm
sector was both extensive and diversified. By any standard
small firms accounted for, at least numerically, the greater
part of all businesses. Small units could be found in
virtually every industry. The Bolton Report emphasised the
extreme variation within the sector in respect of the nature
of the market served, level of resources employed, methods
of operation, efficiency, and the decision making approaches
adopted. Clearly, the selection of a representative sample
of small firms for the South Wessex Survey could not be
straightforward. The Bolton Committee, for example, defined
no fewer than nine major categories of small firms. The
prime sector of interest with which the Bolton Committee was
concerned was manufacturing. This was defined as firms with
up to 200 employees. It is now generally accepted that this
level was probably too high. The South Wessex Survey
concentrated upon small engineering firms only, with an
upper limit of 100 employees. The essence of this decision
was to promote depth of study, and to liaise closely with
Hankinson (1983), given the Bolton assessment of the
multiplicity of the small firm sector.

The sample firms

Eight criteria were adopted to ensure acceptability of the
sample. Different sizes of firm, mechanical and electrical
engineering units, production run capabilities, regional
factors, age, degree of independence, extent of
incorporation, and an acceptable sample size ultimately
determined the 50 firms.

All respondents were interviewed on an open unstructured
personal approach. Follow up interviews were also
undertaken on a continual basis. A feature of this was that
data availability, despite the advent of the microcomputer,
was still a fundamental problem for many small firms. The
South Wessex Survey indicated that the very small firms were
still reluctant to move into computers and even if they did
so the data collection, storage, and accessibility problem
persisted.

Key personnel

The major decisions in most small firms tended to be taken
by a key executive, e.g. the managing director. Others

could be consulted such as co-directors, accountants, and general managers, but the managing director very often dominated decision making. Over 85% of the small firms examined by the Bolton Report in its postal survey were controlled and managed by virtually one man. This key person was the officer who supplied the required data for the South Wessex Survey where the dominance of decision making, if anything, exceeded the 85% Bolton finding.

Although the 'know-how' of these key personnel was considerable, they did not possess high academic qualifications. Detailed information on this topic was not collected, but the Bolton Committee found that 71% of their key personnel had no higher education, 19% possessed accounting or professional qualifications, and only 10% had degrees.

Bolton also published data on the average ages of the chief executives in the small firms under review by the Committee. In the firms with 0-24 employees the average age was 52 years, with 25-99 staff the average was 55, and with 100-199 personnel the mean was 58. It was not the intention of the South Wessex Survey to verify such statistics but the impression was that in the smaller companies promotion to higher management depended more on family ties and less on merit. Not surprisingly, the key person interviewees tended to be older than equivalent key persons in larger companies where merit promotion was more prominent. There were no interviewees in their 20's or early 30's in the sample firms.

Was the quality of decision making affected by qualification, age, etc? This was difficult to test. Many successful small firms were managed by persons with little or no higher education. Conversely there were unsuccessful firms run by relatively well qualified staff. The issue was whether key personnel, qualified or not, could pursue business optimisation policies. There was little evidence to suggest that they had the tools or expertise to aim for other than survival or satisfactory profits at best.

Goals of firms

Interviewees in the South Wessex Survey were asked to state the company's main goal or policy. The principal goal of the firms was survival. Sales growth and satisfactory profit were also prominent. A notable result was the restrained desire to invest, develop new products, diversify, and pursue full capacity working. The Bolton Report demonstrated the innovative role of small firms in a favourable light but that finding now looked over

4

simplified.

It was perhaps not surprising to discover that survival figured significantly in management goals.

It should be noted that mechanical engineering companies comprised 66% of the sample, and electrical engineering firms the remaining 34%. Therefore, any finding resulting in percentages greater or smaller than these could be significant. For example, of the 14 firms concerned with survival 71% were mechanical engineering companies. This must be compared with the below average result of 29% for the electrical engineering firms. Key personnel in the South Wessex Survey gave their reasons for adopting their policies. Several claimed that survival was the only goal for small firms in the light of the 1980's and early 1990's adverse economic conditions. In the main, however, the policy tended to be the result of historical or traditional thinking and not based upon potential.

Conceptions of success

The Bolton Report found that the basic motivation of small firm owners was the need to attain and preserve independence. This desire for independence summarised a whole range of personal requirements provided by self employed working. It took into account numerous qualitative benefits which running a small business provided. These appeared to be much more powerful motivations than financial gain. But the pursuit of survival as a conception of success by over one third of the sample firms suggested a lowering of sights since Bolton. With regard to the companies listing survival as their main conception of success, 72% were mechanical engineering firms, and 28% electrical engineers. Overall it was the smaller firms, i.e. 0-24 employees that considered survival as their major barometer of performance.

Firms considered survival as one of the foundations for profitability. It was possible that survival could have been the fundamental aim since for many small firms it was the only true goal and all other objectives were means of reaching this. A major reason for emphasising survival, apart from the 1980's and early 1990's 'recessions', was that for the majority of managers who made decisions that had significant impact on the activities of the firm, their status and standard of living depended on whether the firm survived or not.

Summary

The South Wessex Survey sample was selected on an eight
tests of acceptability basis. The interviews were conducted
on an open unstructured personal level. To what extent the
quality of decision making was affected by academic
qualifications, age, etc., was not easy to assess, but there
was little evidence to suggest that well qualified managers,
as opposed to unqualified, had the extra expertise to pursue
policies other than those of survival. Firms considered
satisfactory profits and sales growth, second to survival in
the hierarchy of objectives, or as one of the fundamentals
for profitability. It was clear that survival was the
fundamental objective since many firms regarded this as a
barometer of success. The signs were that the firms'
survival mentality adversely affected decision behaviour.

References

Bates, J. A., Lydall, H. F. and Stewart, M. J. (1956). Refer
to *Three Studies on Small Firms*, P. Lund and D. Miner,
Committee of Inquiry on Small Firms Research Report
No. 11, HMSO, p 42.

Bolton, J. E. (1971). *Report of the Committee of Inquiry on
Small Firms* (Bolton Report), Cmnd. 4811, London, HMSO.

Hankinson, A. (1983). *The Investment Problem*, Bournemouth
Polytechnic monograph.

Jervis, F. R. (1957). 'Private Company Finance in the Post-
War Period', *Manchester School*, 25, pp 190-211.

Lund, P. and Miner, D. (1971). 'Comparisons Between Firms of
Different Size Using the CBI Industrial Trends Surveys',
*Committee of Inquiry on Small Firms Research Report No.
11*, HMSO, pp 47-78.

Lund, P. and Miner, D. (1971). 'The Investment Behaviour of
Small Firms', *Committee of Inquiry on Small Firms Research
Report No. 11*, HMSO, pp 83-123.

2 Investment

Investment strategies

If the returns on investment were to be optimised by the small firm, the application of a specific investment strategy would be necessary. Whilst piecemeal approaches to investment could possibly produce short run optimum profit, in the longer term this would be more unlikely. Profit optimisation demands a persistent effort on the part of the decision maker, and this would normally require, among a wide range of techniques and goals, a well defined and implemented investment strategy. This important aspect was investigated in four sections: an assessment of the amount of vertical and horizontal investment that had been undertaken; an analysis of the main investment strategies, if any; how the decision to adopt the various strategies had been reached; and to what extent these strategies had been successful as far as the firms themselves were concerned.

Although difficult to generalise, vertical investment was taken to mean capital expenditure aimed at improvement rather than mere replacement, i.e. horizontal investment. Moreover, vertical and horizontal investment spending refered to the shorter term. Disappointingly, from the point of view of optimality of returns, the majority of the firms adopted the latter policy. There was, however, an indication that the larger units were more inclined towards vertical investment than the smaller firms.

Some firms tended to confuse strategy with short run objectives. A prominent facet of the data was the absence of strategies in 11 firms, i.e. 22% of the sample. This lack of strategic thinking tended to decrease with the increasing size of firm. Piecemeal investment was popularly practised and even where vertical investment strategies were apparent, they had been imposed, in the main, by necessity. There was little evidence of positive investment programming. Indeed, very few of the smaller firms admitted to investment planning ahead beyond 12 months, and many merely invested when the need arose.

It was recorded in Chapter 1 that mechanical engineering firms comprised 66% of the sample, and electrical engineering firms 34%. The results showed that 39 firms (78%) adopted horizontal investment strategies, if indeed, a strategy was in evidence at all. Of these 39 companies, 30 (77%) were in mechanical engineering, and 9 (23%) were electrical engineering concerns. A percentage in excess of 66% for the mechanical engineering group must be regarded as adversely significant, whilst a result below 34% for electrical engineering indicates a more enlightened approach to vertical investment.

At a time of recession throughout the 1980's and early 1990's the mechanical engineering firms had obviously not responded to the need to pursue investment beyond the level of repairs and maintenance. On the other hand, it was likely that the electrical engineering industry had been encouraged to invest in new technology by the rapidly changing nature of the market. But whether the mechanical engineering firms were guilty or not of inadequate investment strategy, finance, appraisal and performance would depend upon further tests and observations.

The 'strategies' employed by the firms could only be regarded as passive. How had they been adopted? What criteria had determined them either in the first instance, or currently? There appeared to be four main areas of strategy derivation: strategies based upon avoidances, strategies determined by the necessity criterion, strategies which simply emerged from historical or traditional application, and strategies pursued for improvement.

Over 50% of the sample had based their strategies on the necessity criterion implying no real positive planning of current and future investment. A further 18% were even more unsure in that the origins of the strategies were shrouded in history or tradition. Seven firms (14%) claimed that their investment strategies had been adopted to avoid either tax or credit. Only 16% were able to state that their investment policies had been thought out to improve profit, productivity, equipment or product.

This 16% representing 8 firms, was small as a sub-sample for analysis, but the data revealed that just 3 firms (38%) were in mechanical engineering, and 5 (62%) in electrical engineering. If the figures were meaningful, the electrical engineering firms appeared to be more inclined to invest positively for improvement than those in mechanical engineering.

The picture seemed fairly clear. Strategies had rarely been pre-planned but had been adopted as a consequence of some specific event or crisis. It was difficult to imagine how these firms could be producing other than survival returns at best over the longer term. Investment strategy need not simply emerge or be non-existent. It could be thought out and applied to avoid the sub-standard returns accruing to the majority of the firms in question. But to what extent did the firms themselves consider that their investment 'strategies' and investment returns had been successful? What levels of investment achievement were acceptable to the firms? How was investment success actually defined or measured? The following gave some points for consideration.

Conceptions of investment success

Conceptions of success of investment strategies, where they existed, covered a wide range and included sustained profits, growth, adequate order books, and increased sales, but mainly survival. Some firms repeated that no investment strategy had ever been employed, yet they too had survived. Were these successes optimal? No firm had actually claimed this. Most were content with satisfactory or survival returns, although some had admitted to disappointing results which might have been avoided if action had been taken at the crucial time, e.g. by prudent bank borrowing. The firms that declared survival as a measure of success were fairly evenly spread between the two sizes of firm used in the study, i.e. 0-24 and 25-100 employees. The impression was that the smaller firm in general was subject to greater vulnerability and survival could indeed be construed as a successful outcome of operating under difficult economic circumstances during the period 1980-1991. These attitudes to investment strategy gave further weight to the likelihood of survival performance only.

It was noteworthy that firms should consider survival as a

conception of success whereas more positive indicators such as profits, sales, growth, order books and product development were much less in evidence.

Moreover, out of the 17 firms quoting survival, 77% were in mechanical engineering, and 23% electrical engineering. The mechanical engineering firms, comprising 66% of the 50 firm sample, were once again over-represented in the holding of somewhat negative attitudes.

Investment and the economic climate

During varying recessionary conditions such as the period 1980-1991 it was perhaps natural for firms to claim that investment was low as a result of future uncertainty. Companies might also argue that output could fall if the rate of inflation at any time was not brought more into line with foreign competitors. Manufacturers could indeed cut back or postpone investment because of bleak growth forecasts and anxieties about the effects of inflation on tight liquidity positions. But did firms take the opposite view when industrial conditions were favourable? During 1980-1991 firms in the South Wessex Survey were asked to specify their main investment problems, the objective being to find out if economic conditions were entirely responsible for sub-optimum investment. If key personnel identified factors other than inflation, government policies, price control, rising wage bills and costs of borrowing, then the remedies could lie more within the firms themselves rather than with central government.

Whilst there was little doubt that a recessionary economic situation affected the decision to invest, it was equally clear that other factors were relevant. When the total 50 population was taken into account, just 38% believed that industrial conditions and the lack of government action were responsible for their investment problems. Although it could be argued that some of the problems other than the economic situation were also outside the control of the firm, many of the difficulties quoted did seem to be self-imposed such as management inexpertise, lack of orders, absence of internal techniques, plant capacity constraints and keeping up with new techniques and developments in that particular industry.

The impression gained was that investment by many of the firms would have been sub-optimum irrespective of the economimc climate. On the other hand, it could be argued that favourable industrial conditions could encourage marginal investment, but perhaps no more than that. Moreover, it must be borne in mind that respondents' answers were first responses only. Thus, the 38% quoted could be slightly understated in the sense that the majority of the firms were unhappy about their perceptions of economic conditions, but did not give this factor top priority in their list of investment hindrances.

A point of interest was perhaps the small degree of importance given to the cost of investment borrowing. But it must be noted that very few firms used borrowing for investment purposes as a specific policy. It was worth noting too that the 19 firms (38%) that quoted the economic situation as the main investment problem were spread fairly evenly between the two employee sized groups 0-24 and 25-100. These firms had particular views about the consequences of worsening economimc trends. And they were supported, of course, to a lesser extent by the other firms that felt that although their difficulties could be attributed to more specific factors, the economic situation could not be dismissed.

Analysing the industrial classifications it was found that of the 19 firms claiming 'uncontrollable external factors' as their main investment problem, 17 firms (89%) were in mechanical engineering, whilst only 2 (10%) were electrical engineers. The electrical engineering sector was, of course, one in which product development was essential to keep pace, whereas the mechanical engineering market tended to be more static. However, it appeared that the mechanical engineering firms over-emphasised the 'uncontrollable external factors' as the root of their investment problems.

Collectively, the South Wessex Survey firms believed that local industry was in some respects subject to certain factors quite beyond the control of individual managements. These factors included fluctuations in world trade supply, prices of raw materials, monetary policies both in the UK and in the countries with whom they traded, increasing government legislation that seemed to be antagonistic to free enterprise and too high an inflation level from the late 1970's to the early 1990's. All these were combining to raise a serious lack of confidence within manufacturing engineering industry particularly when management was faced with decisions regarding future investment. Such feelings persisted despite the numerous measures introduced by the government since 1979 to specifically help the smaller firm.

As a result of these problems, including high interest rates in the late 1980's and early 1990's, several south Wessex firms were working well below capacity. The follow-up visits confirmed that some companies had slimmed down their operations to just 80%, for example, of their former scale. This inevitably was giving rise to greater unemployment, although there was not much evidence of actual redundancies, and short time working. And the trend was beginning to affect even the capital goods and heavy engineering industries where the time lag between receiving orders and the supply was considerable. Despite periodic easings of the situation by the mid-1980's, certain problems had become ingrained in the thinking of small firm management. Every settlement that resulted in wage and salary earners receiving more than the retail price index change, caused further anxiety regarding the loss of jobs. Additionally, because everything that the firms paid for such as labour, materials, fuel, transport, electricity, rates, postal charges, and so on, was increasingly costly, managements were finding it more and more difficult to maintain an adequate level of working capital. It was pointed out by some that if costs rose by, say X%, the management had to correspondingly increase the amount of cash it had available for such purposes as paying wages and purchasing materials simply to maintain the same level of activity before it could even consider increasing output from more capital spending. The majority of companies were quite unable to generate the extra liquidity needed for increased working capital out of their own profits. Consequently, they were forced to seek assistance from the banks although they preferred not to do this. Even if costs of borrowing were relaxed the interest payable on overdrafts could be a burden on the firm's resources and could make it impossible to accept new orders even if available.

The firms in the machine tool and steelwork industries indicated that foreign buyers placing large contracts for capital equipment which could take several years to complete, understandably insisted on fixed prices. Competitors in other countries where inflation rates were lower than in the UK, even though the UK's inflation rate was around 4% in the mid-1980's, could meet this requirement more easily. Firms also admitted that they had turned down orders because they could not forecast their costs accurately enough when inflation was still too high and unpredictable. They felt, too, that foreign competitors' prices were such that insufficient profit could be made to afford the interest charges for the finance required. And they could not be sure of the effects of certain government policies. Generally speaking, most firms in the sample considered that governments had been anti-small firm over the years.

Clearly, it would have been a mistake to have underestimated the economic climate's effect on investment decision making, but at the same time that was by no means the only influence, and in any event the relationship between economic conditions and investment had been shown by Hankinson (1983) to be tenuous. It could have been the case that most small firm industrial investment problems could have been solved more by resolute management rather than by arbitrary economic upturns.

Shorter term investment flexibility

One test of investment effectiveness was the response of capital spending to some important short term development. For example, did small firms invest in accordance with manpower levels? Was investment geared to output changes, or a required level of assets? To what extent had profit prompted investment? It seemed important to examine short run investment behaviour as opposed to capital spending which had been determined largely by longer and perhaps traditional policies, to test optimality. In an attempt to test the flexibility of short run investment decision making, the firms were asked to give examples, if any, where capital expenditure had been undertaken outside the normal patterns of long term investment.

Whilst many of the firms could indicate slight links between labour, output, assets, profit, changes in costs and investment, there was very little evidence to support these relationships over the shorter term despite profit potential. The flexibility normally associated with small firms certainly did not apply to short period capital expenditure, and the lost opportunities could have been considerable. For example, two almost identical firms in the mechanical engineering industry had conflicting views about whether automated processes were possible or not. Other firms said that they would not invest if their own funds were not available, whilst several companies ploughed back into equipment or reserves almost irrespective of requirements. Most firms, however, were aware of the importance of replacement, and depreciation covering in general.

But the main indication was that past profit rather than expected profit led to investment, although rarely in the very short term. To state that investment was low was simply another way of saying that profits were depressed. Profit gave resources for management to expand, and where appropriate, the incentive for investors to provide further liquidity. However, we have already witnessed, for example, that small firms tended not to respond automatically with investment even when the economic climate was favourable. Similarly, investment would not necessarily be high even during periods of relatively high profits. Against this, certain schools of thought might argue that profit was no test of the need for investment. It could be the case that very small firms did not have the will or the vision to

apply flexibility.   However, as far as the South Wessex
Survey firms were concerned, it remained true that provided
that new plant or machinery were required in the normal
course of events, large ex-ante profits were likely to
influence investment far more than any other factor.
Unfortunately, despite the link between profitability and
capital expenditure, short run investment flexibility was
virtually non-existent and this clearly reduced the
prospects for optimum investment and ultimate returns from
that investment.

Longer term visionary investment

Having established a basic relationship between investment
and past profit, although not strong over the very short
period, it would perhaps be misleading to assume that
capital spending was determined by this factor alone.   There
were instances where recent investment had been undertaken
for reasons other than profit availability.   But was this
investment visionary?   Was it investment for the longer run
rather than vertical investment for the shorter term?   If it
could be demonstrated that capital spending had been largely
visionary then chances of investment optimality would be
enhanced.

When touching on investment strategies earlier, it was
noted that when short term vertical and horizontal
investment were observed, only a minority of 12 firms (24%)
had engaged in the former, with 38 firms (76%) in the latter
category.   If the longer term is taken into account then
there is an even more disturbing picture in that only 9
firms (18%) showed evidence of visionary future investment.
The capital spending of 27 companies (54%) was non-visionary
with the smaller firms unfortunately prominent in this
respect.   The remaining 14 (28%) were in a non-classifiable
position.   For example, these 14 firms tended to demonstrate
some evidence of visionary expenditure, but this had been
largely imposed upon them by short run events.

The mechanical engineering firms, once again, were not well
represented in terms of visionary investment, although it
must be said that a sub-sample of 9 firms is too small to be
fully meaningful.   However, only 4 mechanical engineering
companies (44%) could claim sustained visionary investment.
On the other hand 6 electrical engineering firms (66%),
probably pulled along by the nature of the market, had
engaged themselves in anticipatory spending in recent years.

The problem appeared to be an inability on the part of
the small firm to plan long term.   Whilst conclusions were
difficult   to   reach,   the   general   impression   was   that

14

investment optimality was hardly likely if only 18% of the firms had been engaged in visionary investment over recent years. And, of course, there was no guarantee that these firms would continue to invest in this manner over the very long period.

Long term investment planning

Long term investment planning was obviously essential if optimality was to be achieved. Presumably, there was nothing to prevent a firm from ignoring what had happened in the past, or what could reasonably be expected to occur in the future, and still produce a satisfactory performance. But could this performance be sustained long term? If firms sought out long term indicators which could influence current investment, and paid serious attention to them, then the achievement of attainable investment levels and investment returns would be more likely than if those indicators were ignored. Firms in the South Wessex Survey were asked to specify which indicators, if any, helped to form general investment expectations for the future.

Judging from the responses it was clear that very few firms used likely future indicators as specific influences on their investment decisions. Many firms felt that no reliable indicators existed and, for example, considered themselves unavoidably conditioned by their industry's trends. However, some firms had obviously appraised possible future developments, but whether investment had actually taken place in response to this was arguable.

Although perhaps all firms had their investment thinking influenced by economic indicators at some time or other, the responses suggested that the link between current investment and likely future trends was not strong. Some 52% of the sample merely used historical data, short run market trends (although not necessarily guaranteeing short run investment), or claimed that no indicators were available, or employed. Both employee group sizes (0-24 and 25-100) were well represented in this respect.

Further analysis revealed that out of the 17 firms actually recognising long term investment indicators, 11 (65%) were in mechanical engineering, and 6 (35%) in electrical engineering. With electrical engineering firms comprising 33% of the entire sample, a 35% result above would indicate, if only marginally, that these firms were ignoring the value of long term planning rather more than the mechanical engineering firms. A possible defence of this could be that since 'electronics' was advancing at a rapid pace and the longer term was legitimately an unknown factor,

15

with mechanical engineering that argument could not be applied to the same extent.

Only 16% of the sample had considered improved government capital spending incentives to be helpful, a result which coincided markedly with the general disillusionment with investment incentives generally. The phasing out of these incentives in the late 1980's was probably long overdue. Yet it was repeatedly pointed out by the respondents that one of the main determinants of investment was funds available from profit. If costs, for example, were reduced giving more surplus funds, the chances were that investment would respond over the longer term. But clearly, firms were not enthusiastic about government assistance in this area despite the numerous measures announced by the government between 1980 and 1991 to help the smaller business unit.

In general terms one had to conclude from the findings that long term investment planning was nominal, and the contribution which such an approach could make towards investment optimality was equally constrained.

Investment determinants and influences

One of the main features of the small business unit was the lack of complexity in its management structure. The average small firm in the South Wessex Survey was managed by its owners who took nearly all the important decisions. Indeed, it will be remembered that the Bolton Report (1971) confirmed that over 85% of small firms in its postal survey were controlled and managed by one or two men, and usually one. This direct dependence on the proprietor was striking, and constituted both a source of strength and weakness for the the small firm. For example, it accounted for the occasional rapidity of decision making, it made for employee morale, and ensured that the pursuit of solvency was not relaxed. On the other hand the skills and expertise of any one individual in the small firm sector was demonstrably limited. The running of a small business by experience and commonsense could be effective so long as the scale of the firm's activities and the pressures from outside remained undemanding. But optimality would not necessarily follow. And, as indicated, even if scales of operation and outside pressures were manageable, profit was likely to be below par as a result of doubtful investment strategies, if any, and self-imposed investment problems hindered by unfavourable economic uncertainties.

The vital question could now be posed. How was the decision to invest actually reached, and which factors determined and influenced investment in the firms under review?

The responses tended to be specific to each individual firm, but four main areas could be indentified. Investment determined by necessity. Investment determined by the desire to improve returns. Investment determined by finance. And investment determined by miscellaneous factors.

The main determinant of investment was the need to invest in new plant or machinery as a result of some pressing factor or event, e.g. urgent replacement investment, investment to comply with safety regulations, and so on. Indeed, sheer necessity represented some 46% of the total responses, and both employee group sizes of 0-24 and 25-100 were fairly equally represented.

A characteristic of these results was that only 6% of the sample regarded the rate of return or yield as a major determinant of investment. Past profits were far more significant, a result confirmed later under the heading of Investment Flexibility. Capital spending was likely to proceed even if the yield was below target, provided that the investment item was actually required, and that own funds were available, or the cost of borrowing was not prohibitive, in which case, the investment would be postponed. The cost of borrowing and bank credit comprised only 8% of the responses. This hardly suggested the pursuit of investment optimisation. In fact, where investment had been rendered imperative, firms had simply responded almost irrespective of the consequences.

When firms were given a second choice there was a definite shifting of emphasis towards the cost of borrowing and bank credit availability, but it must be noted that these were regarded as mere influences of investment rather than determinants. Even so, it was disappointing to find that only 18% felt that government investment incentives were of any significance in their investment decisions.

If firms undertook investment then it would normally be assumed that they did this to obtain a return, the ultimate objective being long term profit. However, the South Wessex Survey showed that once the decision to invest had been reached, usually based upon need and past profits available, the rate of return appeared to be of subsidiary importance. Again, very little evidence of investment optimisation was apparent here.

As far as influences were concerned, these merely reflected investment decisions. For example, once capital spending had been agreed, then the decision could have been influenced, but not necessarily postponed, by the cost of borrowing, bank credit availability, government incentives, past profit, rival investment, length of order books, industry trends and the economic climate. Investment decisions should not preferably proceed in this manner. Legitimate reasons for visionary investment should be identified and acted upon. The findings showed that 24 firms based their actual investment decisions on the necessity criterion. Out of these 24 companies, 17 (71%) were in mechanical engineering, and 7 (29%) in electrical engineering. The 29% for the latter was favourably significant and could possibly be explained in terms of that industry's rapid development, and the pressure on firms to have no other choice but to keep pace as of necessity or lose ground.

Despite all this, it might still be argued that firms investing in response to some need or marginal influence, did this because they thought it would bring long term benefits. This was never in dispute. The issue under review here was whether investment levels and investment returns were optimum or not. It seemed likely from the evidence that they were not.

Summary

There was little evidence of positive investment thinking in that 78% of short run capital expenditure was horizontal. Very few of the firms admitted to planning ahead and merely invested when the need arose. Of the not inconsiderable number of firms that declared survival as a measure of success, the split between the 0-24 and 25-100 employee groups was fairly even. General attitudes to investment strategy gave weight to the survival hypothesis. Whilst there was little doubt that a recessionary economic climate affected the decision to invest, it was equally clear that other, and perhaps more basic, factors were relevant. In most cases individual investment problems could have been tackled more by resolute management than by arbitrary economic upturns. Whilst many of the firms could indicate links between the selected variables, (labour, output, asset levels, and profits) and investment, there was little evidence to support these relationships over the shorter period. Despite a strong link between past profit and capital expenditure, short run investment flexibility was virtually non-existent and this clearly reduced the prospects of optimum investment and optimum investment returns. Investment optimality was likely to be impaired as a result of non-visionary capital spending by the vast majority of the sample firms. And it was notable that the mechanical engineering firms were far more guilty of this deficiency than the electrical engineering companies. Very few firms used likely future indicators as specific influences on their investment decisions, and many considered that no reliable indicators existed. Long term investment planning was nominal and the contribution such a policy could have made towards investment optimality was equally limited. Investment was determined mainly by necessity or crisis which rendered capital spending imperative, provided that the firm's own funds were available. The cost of borrowing, credit availability, and government investment incentives were revealed to be mere influences of investment only.

References

Bolton, J. E. (Chairman). (1971). *Small Firms: Report of the Committee of Inquiry on Small Firms*, November, Cmnd. 4811.

Hankinson, A. (1983). *The Investment Problem*, Bournemouth Polytechnic monograph.

3 Finance

Sources of investment finance

The Merrett Cyriax Survey (1971), a research report for the
Bolton Committee (1971), found that in manufacturing
industry no less than 92% of the firms in their sample had
not been concerned in any attempt to obtain finance through
financial institutions other than their local bank. Three
reasons were given for this. Firms did not seek finance
because they did not need it. Firms would not seek finance
through ignorance, prejudice, or moral scuples. For
example, 40% of the respondents felt that it was unethical
to borrow capital. And firms could not obtain finance
because they were not credit worthy. Merrett Cyriax
concluded that self-financing remained the dominant
financial characteristic of the small firm sector. This
finding in 1971 remained true in the late 1980's and early
1990's despite the many alternative sources of finance for
small businesses available. The Bolton Committee (1971)
found that bank credit formed the greater part of external
finance for small firms (63% of the sample had overdrafts)
and the use of bank credit appeared to increase with the

size of firm. Bolton also found that fast growing manufacturing firms in their sample showed greater reliance on bank borrowing, a fast growing firm being defined as one in which sales grew by 15% or more per year at current prices. A slow growing firm was defined as one in which sales remained stationary, or declined, and these had less recourse to external borrowing than the fast growers.

In the South Wessex Survey, 36% of the firms had reluctantly used banking facilities for investment purposes when their own, or private, funds had been inadequate. The two major groups in the sample, i.e. mechanical engineering and electrical engineering, showed a remarkable similarity of preference for their own funds and/or bank finance for investment purposes. Some 73% of the mechanical engineering firms preferred their own funds, and 67% had had to resort to bank finance. In the electrical engineering group the figures were 65% and 70% respectively. A minority of firms in both groups had opted for other sources such as private loans. Where firms had obtained funds from the parent company or group, it was difficult to establish whether this had, in turn, been provided externally. Practically all the firms had a bank overdraft but this was considered to be normal business practice and did not compare with the acquisition of funds from the various other institutions. Nevertheless, firms with overdrafts stressed that even those had been obtained with some reluctance during the period of high interest rates and general recession of the 1980's and early 1990's. Thus, the tendency was to increasingly resist bank lending and this was regarded as important by the respondents. It seemed obvious that a large part of the firms' long term finances for investment had been provided by owners' capital, profits, and private loans, with bank support a last resort.

Without doubt firms preferred to use their own funds for investment purposes. Some 40% of the sample opted for this source. Some companies were emphatic about rejecting excessive credit even if potentially profitable. Others pointed out the importance of profit or track record if bank facility had to be resorted to. Why did the firms reject the principle of external funds? Why did they, in the main, prefer not to incur excessive credit even though possibly profitable? Was this 'survival' attitude based upon the difficulties of raising finance in the past? The firms in question were asked to give this issue some consideration in view of the Bolton Committee's (1971) initial finding that firms that had relied on bank finance had grown faster than those that had not used this source, or had used it to a lesser extent. And, of course, it was important in the sense that this reluctance to employ bank credit was likely to impair the optimisation of investment levels and

21

investment returns.

Difficulties in the raising of investment finance

The firms were asked to recall the difficulties, if any,
which had been experienced in the raising of funds for
investment purposes. An interesting aspect of these
findings concerned the firms that claimed to have had
difficulties when raising finance. It appeared that the
problem was inversely related to the size of firm in that
the smaller ones were more critical of the banks' 'unhelpful
attitudes'. Only a small number of firms (6%) had had no
difficulty whatever in the raising of funds, yet 10% had not
even explored the possibility of bank finance for
investment.
Did the banks discriminate against certain firms? Analysis
showed that 36% of the firms in mechanical engineering and
29% in electrical engineering claimed that they had
experienced some difficulty in the acquisition of funds from
the banks for investment. When the two groups were taken
together, the firms that were neither specialists nor geared
to large production runs, appeared to have suffered the
most. Some 46% claimed this to be the case. Just how many
firms of this 46% could present a loan proposal to the bank
in an acceptable manner was difficult to judge. It should
be remembered that of the firms not inconvenienced by the
banks, many had adopted a non-borrowing policy, and had
tended to set their investment sights low. No large scale
investment programmes had been undertaken and consequently
the need for excessive capital finance had not arisen.
Nevertheless, 38% (not counting the 6% above) of the sample
claimed to have had no major problems when raising finance
for investment equipment up to 1991. Was there a limit to
this success? Could firms have raised additional finance
and, provided that the investment was basically sound,
reaped the profits? Were firms in favour of utlising bank
credit for future returns?
A small percentage of the firms had had difficulty, but for
individual reasons, e.g. new firm becoming established,
recessionary conditions during the 1980's and 1990's,
seasonal trade effects, finance for experimental necessity,
and so on. But a significant result, reinforcing an
emerging trend, was that a good survival profit record was
the real key to the raising of finance. Many of the firms
preferred to use their own funds rather than resort to any
form of external finance. In most cases they were unaware
of the potential sources of funds. For many of the firms
finance had probably been available for investment from

outside sources, but they seemed to have been reluctant to take advantage of it. A number of respondents chose to attack the banks for failing to understand seasonal problems, and many felt that these institutions should only be approached as a last resort if, indeed, a policy of borrowing was in operation at all. Some believed that if a major investment were undertaken and a large outlay was involved, then real problems of raising the finance would emerge, especially since borrowing powers were strongly related to profitability rather than performance potential.

Many of the firms could be criticised for their non-positive approach to investment finance. Loan finance does not necesarily lead to losses. It would most likely promote profitability if the investment proposal had been accorded the usual careful considerations beforehand. Several companies outlined opportunities for expansion and improvement, but still preferred the status quo. Some visionary investment via the institutions could well have taken advantage of the very opportunities identified by the firms themselves. Levels of capital expenditure, and the eventual investment returns were falling short of optimum. What exactly were the reasons for the firms' reluctance to resort to institutional finance, possibly at the expense of profitability? At this point, and especially now that the role of the bank manager has changed, attention may now be focussed on the question of external finance.

External finance

Generally speaking industry had faced an investment dilemma over the years. The private small firm sector, often criticised for perennially low investment, appeared to require more and more official encouragement before undertaking further fixed capital formation. South Wessex firms, however, felt that the lessons of recession since 1980 had taught that a cautious approach to investment was often preferable to an immediate response to government exhortation or the provision of investment funds. And as already pointed out even buoyant demand and reflationary economic conditions did not always lead to increased short run investment.

The government's reaction to falling investment intentions had been twofold. The first was covered by the view that if private industries would not invest, then the government should do it for them. This belief found its embodiment in such enterprises as the National Enterprise Board, but the south Wessex firms considered such institutions further reduced business confidence and were consequently counter-productive. The second reaction concerned incentives in annual budgets. Apart from the problem of small firms' lack of will to invest, there had always been the lack of means argument. The government's introduction of measures, and especially since 1980, to assist the small firm sector, was obviously designed to ease the problem. Unfortunately, many of the south Wessex firms were either unaware of the measures, or declared them to be not applicable, or totally inadequate.

There was no real shortage of external finance sources, but it was evident that the firms did not, in the main, resort to these funds. The impression was that external finance, not unlike ordinary bank credit, was to be avoided. Why was this the case when outside finance could have led to profit?

A feature of the answers to these questions was that 94% of the south Wessex firms had not been involved in any attempt to secure finance through facilities beyond the local bank or other related sources. The Merrett Cyriax Survey (1971) had also found similarly with a 92% response. Hankinson (1977) produced a figure of 95%

Some 36% of the sample claimed that they had not required external finance, and in any event, would have used their own funds or overdrafts. Just under 30% felt that they should avoid external credit in order to preserve a measure of independence, believing that outside finance was synonymous with outside control. A large number of the firms made this point and it must be regarded as the major reason for the rejection of external funds, but 28% were particularly trenchant on this issue. Surprisingly, 14% of the sample, mainly the smaller firms, were not too familiar with institutional sources, the procedures, or their own credit standing.

Could profits have been increased if external funds had been used for investment? There is little doubt that the institutions ensure that a venture is profitable before funds are made available, and especially if a 10% control is undertaken. Thus, it might reasonably be assumed that profits were being lost by firms' refusals to resort to these funds. In other words, firms appeared to be content with an investment finance situation that could conceivably have contributed to sub-optimum investment levels, and sub-optimum investment returns.

Role of government

British industry over the years tended to lack the capacity on the one hand, and the investment in technology on the other, to play its full part in market development and expansion. The question was, and still is but perhaps to a lesser extent in the late 1980's and early 1990's, how this could be brought about? Industry generally and the small firm sector in particular, seemed reluctant to take the initiative. The impression was that governments had to set the pace.

But to what degree did small firms actually react to government decisions? For example, to what extent was investment decision making adversely affected by government policy, and what did small firms expect from government? How did changes in the base rate and credit availability impact on investment finance decisions? And importantly, how were investment decisions influenced by the various incentives made available by government?

About 10% of the south Wessex firms believed that excessive bureaucratic demands by governments were a disincentive to investment activity within the firm. Some 16% considered that high taxation, rent and rates, and especially the new uniform business rate from 1990, were major problems, despite the fact that small firms, in the main, should have paid little or no tax. Just 8% felt that governments over-intervened generally, but a total of 32% were convinced that a lack of positive government intervention, e.g. the inability to control recessionary economic conditions, was the real key to the problem of low investment. It was not too surprising to find that only 6% complained of high rates of interest since many of the firms had actually adopted a non-borrowing philosophy over recent years. However, there was far more concern about interest rates during 1990 and 1991.

Five of the firms (10%) dealt directly or indirectly with the government itself. They complained of the lack of contracts. It was felt that such work, if placed more often, would stimulate investment. However, the impression was that contracts were probably not being tendered for correctly or even adequately.

A mere 2% said that government incentives were, or had been, reasonable, but 24% declared that government assistance was quite often inappropriate, inadequate or non-existent. It must be said, again, that many of the firms were simply unaware of the numerous measures introduced by the government to help small businesses during the period 1980-1991.

Further analysis revealed that the smaller firms were the ones claiming to be more affected by high taxation, government bureaucratic demands and inflation, for example, in the early 1980's, than their larger counterparts. Moreover, out of the 12 firms declaring government aid to be usually inappropriate, inadequate, or even non-existent, 10 (83%) were in the mechanical engineering industry, and only

2 (17%) in electrical engineering. Yet the 1 firm expressing satisfaction with government assistance was also in mechanical engineering. If only 6% of the firms claimed that they were not affected by government policy, then what did the remaining 94% actually expect from governments?

Expectations of government

What were the most important areas of improvement that the government could implement, and which might raise investment expectations within small firms? An ambivalent attitude could be discerned in that on the one hand the south Wessex firms had repeatedly valued their independence, e.g. by rejecting external finance and the possibility of external control, whilst on the other, they clearly expected some assistance from the authorities. And this was true despite the 20% that felt governments should intervene less.

If governments had to intervene then 48% of the firms felt that assistance should be direct, such as the abolition of small firm taxation in favour of ploughback, the placing of more contracts, the introduction of a concessionary borrowing rate and the further reduction of bureaucratic demands. Indirect monetary assistance, e.g. credit availability, was not regarded as significant. The impression was that most of the firms considered such assistance as the Loan Guarantee Scheme, Business Expansion Scheme, employment protection measures and the advisory services, as far less important than, say, the placing of direct contracts by government departments.

Out of the 10 firms opting for less government intervention, 6 (60%) were in mechanical engineering. Since this industry appeared to be most affected by recessions, one might suspect that this response was more of a protest than a request. As expected, the 5 companies (50%) that also indicated the need for less intervention were one-off specialists, firms rather less affected by adverse conditions. The 7 firms (14%) demanding concessionary borrowing rates were, again, in mechanical engineering. On the other hand, and not surprisingly, only 2 of the 13 specialist one-off firms felt that such a concession would be helpful.

Thus, it was confirmed that small firms' investment was, in the main, more likely to respond to government action if it impacted directly on profitability rather than policies that promised indirect, delayed, or unidentifiable financial assistance. Whilst firms agreed that increased profits would most likely result in increased investment ultimately, they also stressed the need for confidence and market stability, and these had to be inspired by government.

This distinction between direct and indirect assistance could be an important issue for government policy. The literature is not very prominent in this area, although Hankinson (1978) drew attention to it. If firms emphasised the importance of direct and immediate financial assistance, an item of some concern was whether monetary policy, so prominent during the 1980's, was as successful as the government in question presumed. Had bank credit manipulation been an effective influence on investment? Did reductions in the base rate promote capital expenditure in small firms? And was there any evidence that changes in the old minimum lending rate (effectively abolished in 1981) actually affected investment? But first, how helpful were the banks in the eyes of the small firm?

Effectiveness of the banks

It has already been established that small firms preferred their own funds to bank credit whenever possible. One reason for this was adverse economic conditions reducing expected yields. Given this general background of recession and reduced expectations, had the banks been helpful to firms with their problems?

Only 4 firms (8%) had found the banks consistently helpful. Banks were accused of being unhelpful, when conditions were adverse by 9 firms (18%), in demanding excessive security by 10 firms (20%), in over-stressing track record rather than potential by 7 firms (14%) and in taking too few risks by 11 firms (22%). It was possible that these views were to some extent extreme. The banks themselves argued that they had responded to the needs of the smaller firm since the Wilson Report (1979) called for more measures favouring this sector of industry. Even if a case could be made in defence of the banks, the fact remained that over 90% of the firms in question were dissatisfied, in some way, if not totally, with the services offered by the banks. This was disturbing since the banks did play a crucial role in the financing of small firms, providing at least two thirds of their funds, including overdrafts.

Perhaps in summary one could quote Bannock (1981). In his article Bannock confirmed that small business interests complained that banks would not even assume normal commercial risks in lending while charging excessive premia. Moreover, bank managers once vested with discretion and responsibility were then subservient to regional offices that knew little about local conditions and even less about the borrower's business. The banks responded that much of their lending was unsecured, that no demonstrably viable business was refused finance and that small business proprietors frequently lacked the necessary financial controls and skills to present their case properly. They also said that in many cases what a small firm really needed was not loan capital but equity.

It may well be that whilst neither side had much hard evidence to support its case, the confusion, suspicion, and mistrust, prevailed.

Effects of government credit control

The decade 1970-1980 was an interesting one for it contained wide degrees of credit control. In 1970 the original monetary policy rules were in force, including stop-go. By the end of 1971 the rules were reversed and credit availability via the market mechanism was in operation, and expansion continued throughout 1972. However, a tightening up of the system could be discerned during 1973. The beginnings of a return to the old controls emerged during 1974. By early 1975 the full circle was complete, and monetary control continued into the 1980's. Thus, throughout the 1970's, 1980's and early 1990's south Wessex firms had experienced control and market freedom. Had their investment planning been affected by the varying degrees of credit availability during this time? To what extent was monetary policy an effective stimulation of investment in small firms?

The results showed that credit availability or control, i.e. easy or restricted funds, had had no or marginal effect on 74% of the sample, and where some influence was apparent in 26% of the population, this had occurred only under special conditions. A significant feature was that 12% of the firms felt that credit control would only be effective if severe over the longer term. Investment which had to be postponed due to a shortage of funds, would simply be undertaken at a later date if conditions eased. Similarly, if finance were made freely available, this in itself would be no determinant of investment. If firms had traditionally maintained a low level of borrowing or had not required funds on large scale, and 22% of the firms were in this category, then government credit manipulation was likely to have negligible effects on those companies. And if investment was regarded as crucial, e.g. repairs and maintenance, then this spending would have to proceed and the funds acquired from alternative sources. Thus, the impression was that investment in these firms was unlikely to be influenced by limited monetary policy designed to regulate the amount of credit availability.

On the other hand, 26% of the sample set out conditions under which their investments might be significantly or seriously affected. If credit were not available, then this could inhibit capital spending, but only in the short run. In other words, this response reinforced the view that mild credit control was non-effective in the longer period. However, if the control were severe and sustained, which was unlikely, then 12% of the firms believed that this would certainly affect investment. The total picture indicated that if governments wished to stimulate investment in manufacturing industry, then the implementation of monetary policy should be awarded low priority unless generous and persistent.

Firms were not exactly optimising their investment activities in relation to credit manipulation by the authorities. On the one hand firms would invest if they considered it necessary to do so irrespective of credit conditions. In this sense the firm could be seen to be pursuing investment opportunities against the constraints and thus optimising. On the other hand, it was clear that the release of credit had done little to actually increase real investment. Firms had simply invested as required and had not taken advantage of easy credit facilities. Indeed, several firms confirmed, yet again, that they avoided excessive credit as a policy in the belief that borrowing was something to avoid. A few firms had turned to factoring, hire purchase or leasing. Other companies complained that credit had not been available when most needed, and that was on start-up. Were there any lessons for governments here? The results suggested that the promotion of investment in small firms appeared to require rather more than the mere manipulation of credit levels.

Investment and the cost of borrowing

In August 1981 the practice of continuously posting the minimum lending rate was discontinued, though the authorities reserved the right to announce in advance the minimum lending rate which, for a short period ahead, the Central Bank would apply to any lending in the market. In future the Bank would aim to keep interest rates at the very short end of the market within an undisclosed band which would be moved from time to time. It would rely mainly on open market operations, i.e. the buying and selling of bills, rather than on direct lending.

Whether the cost of borrowing was determined as a minimum lending rate or as a market rate was not in itself too serious a point. What was important was that the level of investment and the cost of borrowing had been traditionally considered to be inversely related. A high rate would contract investment, a low one would expand it. Over the years governments traded on this assumption in frequent movements in the minimum lending rate to catalyse changes in the economy. Commentators doubted the strength of the minimum lending rate for this purpose, e.g. the Radcliffe Report (1959). How relevant was this theory in the real world and would a persistently low rate of interest actually stimulate investment by small firms?

The question produced some complicated answers, but a fairly clear cut overall result from the south Wessex firms emerged. The responses could be grouped into three sections:

Investment would remain constant, if the rate change
   was marginal only, if the project was vital and
   if future yields were not too unpredictable.

Investment would fall, if the rate rose significantly
   from any level, if the project was not vital and if
   the outlay was large.

Investment would rise, if the rate fell significantly,
   if the lower rate persisted longer term, if future
   yields were predictable and if the project was
   re-defined as vital.

Clearly, a time lag problem arose before any investment cut back was restored to the original level at the original rate of interest. This could possibly explain why real investment in manufacturing industry throughout the 1970's and much of the 1980's never exceeded the 1970 level. The rate could change quickly but investment took time to recover, and especially so in the smaller firm.

It was worth noting that very few of the firms were aware of the problems associated with calculating the cost of capital. Firms had paid little attention to their costs of capital and this had hindered the investment decision to go ahead.

It was possible that the greatest impact of a change in the rate of interest on investment was through its psychological influence on expectations. Because the rate of interest could not be relied upon as a direct determinant of investment, its use as a monetary weapon had to be for other reasons, chiefly external to attract funds from abroad and to restore international confidence, and internal through its psychological effect on industry generally. Certainly, the investment behaviour of the south Wessex firms with regard to the cost of borrowing appeared to be both involved and unpredictable. If the cost of borrowing were reduced to a previous level where investment had occurred, and now firms were reluctant to proceed then it could mean that the companies in question were unable to invest for a variety of reasons, e.g. lack of funds. On the other hand, it might be the case that firms were reluctant to proceed on the grounds that the expected yields were considered to be lower than the cost of borrowing. The impression was that if the cost of borrowing was linked specifically with the level of investment then the latter was probably the case.

But how were these yields actually assessed? If, for example, the calculations were non-rigorous, and it was suspected that this was the case, then firms were in danger of losing occasional cheap finance, and ultimate profit. Of course, one could argue that if calculations were crude it would be equally possible to make the right decision as the wrong one. It was known that small firms tended to be over-cautious as far as investment was concerned. If the investment appraisal yield emerged as high, then the safety margin in operation could still prevent the project going ahead. And if the yield were lower than the cost of borrowing then the investment would be held back. This whole question of investment appraisal is taken up in Chapter 4.

At this stage it may be strongly inferred that monetary policy involving nominal changes in the cost of borrowing, e.g. downwards to raise investment, has not enjoyed notable neasures of success, and the authorities were wise to withdraw the posting of the minimum lending rate in August 1981.

Investment incentives

For some time, and especially since 1980 up to 1985, government investment incentives relevant to the south Wessex small firms had been available, and improved. Had the firms taken advantage of these to boost investment and profit? Had their investment strategies been influenced in any way by the provision of loan schemes, tax incentives, advisory services, easier employment measures, and reduced bureaucratic demands?

Only 6% of the sample, the very small firms not at all, could claim that investment incentives of all kinds had had a significant and direct influence on their capital expenditure decisions.

Although 50% of the firms said that their investment plans

could be encouraged by incentives they regarded this
influence as marginal, and the smaller firms again
predominated here.

The investment decisions of 44% of the sample had clearly
not been influenced in any way by government incentives
between 1980 and 1991. The phasing out of allowances from
the mid-1980's was clearly inevitable. Indeed, many of the
firms were simply not aware of the government's measures.
And those firms that were aware, felt that they were too
little and too late. These findings compare interestingly
with Hankinson (1978) where it was held that regional aid,
for example, was only 9% effective.

Of the firms claiming not to have been influenced at all by
incentives, 70% were in mechanical engineering. Of the 26
firms admitting a marginal influence only, 60% of these
were, again, mechanical engineers. Since this industry
appeared to have been most affected by recessionary
conditions, it was surprising that it had not taken more
advantage of the assistance offered. It was difficult to
understand the firms' ignorance of such aid at any time.
These findings were considered to be of some importance.
Incentives were designed to ease the financial problems of
firms in the encouragement of industrial investment, and the
creation of employment in certain instances. But the
majority of the south Wessex firms were obviously only
interested in incentives when they actually coincided with
their own plans for investment. If firms were investment
optimising, then presumably they would be incentive
optimising also. This was clearly not the case - a somewhat
disturbing result from the point of view of government
policy. Even more important was why this situation should
prevail.

An apparent paradox within the findings above and the
results obtained in Chapter 2 was that on the one hand firms
ignored incentives for investment purposes whilst on the
other hand they had specifically claimed that a major
determinant of capital expenditure was profitability.
Assuming that incentives were a means of supplementing
profit, why should firms reject this assistance? The
reasons given for this by the south Wessex firms were that
aid was not always available for the purpose intended, the
firms could not always raise the additional finance required
to complement the assistance from government, large scale
investment had not been undertaken and thus help was not
needed, aid was regarded as a bonus after the decision to
invest had been reached and the claiming of aid was far too
bureaucratically invloved.

Yet despite the evidence and the alleged weaknesses of the
incentives procedure it would be misleading to conclude that
the UK system discriminated against small firms. Incentives

were available and the south Wessex firms had, in the main, declined to take full advantage of them. As a consequence it was hardly likely that the companies under review were optimising their investment activities as far as incentives were concerned. The phasing out of incentives in favour of lower taxation by the authorities in the late 1980's was clearly inevitable and possibly long overdue.

Summary

Finance for investment had been provided almost equally by the firms' own funds and bank credit with some reluctance. Some companies were emphatic about rejecting excessive credit even if potentially profitable. For many of the firms in the sample, finance was usually available, and difficulties capable of solution, but they seemed slow to take advantage of outside credit facilities. Several firms had adopted a non-borrowing policy. Some 94% of the south Wessex firms had not been concerned in any attempt to obtain finance through facilities beyond the local bank or other subsidiary sources, believing that such credit was a threat to their independence. There was also a general lack of awareness of these sources. Nearly one third of the sample was convinced that lack of government intervention, e.g. the inability to control recessionary conditions, was the key to low investment. Small firms' investment was more likely to respond to government action which impacted directly on profitability rather than policy which provided indirect, delayed, or unidentified financial assistance. Government policies of credit control operating through the monetary sector had achieved very little in increasing long run investment. For three quarters of the firms, such policies had had nil, or only marginal, effect. A rising cost of borrowing appeared to reduce capital expenditure more than a falling cost of borrowing would increase it. Monetary policy involving nominal changes in the cost of borrowing to influence investment favourably, had not enjoyed, and was unlikely to enjoy, notable degrees of success, and the authorities had been wise to withdraw the posting of the minimum lending rate in August 1981. Only 6% of the survey firms could claim that incentives of all kinds had had a significant effect on their capital spending decisions. Some incentives were still available, despite certain anomalies in the system, but firms had, in the main, declined to avail themselves of them. The phasing out of incentives in favour of lower taxation by the government in the late 1980's was inevitable. As a result of all this it was likely that the companies under review were not optimising their investment finances, and especially those in mechanical engineering.

References

Bannock, G. (1981). 'The Clearing Banks and Small Firms', *Lloyds Bank Review*, October, No. 142.

Bolton, J. E. (Chairman). (1971). *Small Firms: Report of the Committee of Inquiry on Small Firms*, Cmnd. 4811.

Hankinson, A. (1977). 'The Investment Behaviour of the Smaller Manufacturing Business Unit 1974-1977', *University of Bath*.

Hankinson, A. (1978). 'How Effective is Regional Aid?' *Management Accounting*, January, Vol. 56 (1), p 17.

Merrett Cyriax Associates, (1971). 'Dynamics of Small Firms', *Committee of Inquiry on Small Firms Research Report No. 12.* November, HMSO.

Radcliffe, (1959) 'The Radcliffe Report on the Working of the Monetary System', *The Radcliffe Report*, HMSO.

Wilson, H. (Chairman). (1979). 'The Financing of Small Firms: Interim Report of the Committee to Review the Functioning of the Financial Institutions', *The Wilson Report*, HMSO.

4 Appraisal

Introduction

An efficient and accurate means of appraising the
worthwhileness of prospective investment is obviously
essential for a firm which seeks to optimise profits where
all investments do not yield the same returns over the same
period of time. The substitution of other objectives for
that of optimality does not, however, negate the need for
accurate investment appraisal since it is virtually
impossible to justify an intended investment subjectively
except in circumstances where the potential economic returns
are immaterial.

It remains surprising, therefore, how little attention has
been paid to this area of a firm's operations within the
United Kingdom. One might postulate a possible connection
between the unscientific approach to investment appraisal
and the slow rate of growth of the British post-war economy
during which period the vast bulk of published data on this
subject has appeared. The evidence suggests that most firms
have concentrated exclusively upon the 'traditional' methods
of appraisal namely variants of the pay-back method

or the rate of return on capital employed method. These two approaches to investment appraisal have been viewed in an unfavourable light principally on the grounds that they are either inaccurate, too conservative, or both, when compared with 'modern' techniques such as the internal rate of return or net present value.

How were the South Wessex Survey firms' investment projects actually calculated for viability? Were any of the discounting techniques employed? How were cash flows assessed? How had the methods of investment appraisal and cash flow assessment been selected for use by the firms? Were any special factors, e.g. tax, risk, etc., taken into account in the calculations, and if so, how? To what extent did the firms improve their methods of appraisal? And which major management techniques did the firms use generally? Thus, the objective of Chapter 4 was to assess investment optimality at the appraisal stage.

Calculation of investment projects

In general terms discounting methods of investment appraisal have the obvious important advantage that they take into account the time pattern of cash flows and the cost of finance. Other methods which do not take into account both of these factors must be considered to be inferior for most purposes. An exception to this, of course, could be that sometimes there might be a reason of overriding importance for investment which would make a precise evaluation of costs and return by any method inappropriate. Nevertheless, whilst rule of thumb investment appraisal techniques could be more than adequate for small firms on most occasions, over the longer term some profitable ventures could be missed. Of course, even if every firm did adopt rigorous approaches to appraisal it is not suggested that all investments would reap maximum profits. But firms would clearly be more aware, for example, of the advantage of having cash flow monitored.

Bearing this in mind, how did the sample firms calculate their investment projects? The findings were difficult to summarise. The complications arose as a result of the way in which some answers were given. For example, where firms were asked which method of investment appraisal they employed, basically two types of response emerged. A specific method would be quoted such as payback, or certain qualifications would accompany the first named technique, e.g. payback was employed but net present value was adopted for major projects and occasionally as a checking device. This whole aspect of investment appraisal must be regarded as a fairly vital area of debate and the results require comment. It was suspected at the hypothesis stage that small firms did not employ rigorous investment appraisal techniques or calculation and this was certainly confirmed. But it must be noted that the rate of return or payback, however ascertained, was not always the crucial factor, e.g. when the 'necessity criterion' was applied. It is probably true to state that where firms adopted trial and error methods these tended to be suitable and adequate for their purpose. This is not to say, of course, that such an approach would be wise for larger and more committed business units.

The findings indicated that the traditional methods were by far the most popular used by the firms. Some 44% of the sample relied upon these simpler techniques. Only 8% used discounted cash flow (DCF) either mainly, or occasionally, as a checking device or for major projects only. A notable feature was the absence of formal calculation by 48% of the sample, and the smaller firms predominated (64%) here. But a most surprising result was the 28% that claimed to be totally unaware of the mechanics of DCF. Nearly 40% of the smaller, and 12% of the larger firms admitted to this.

Much of the South Wessex Survey findings are supported by Hankinson (1979) where in a survey of 65 small companies employing up to 200 people in manufacturing industry in the south west Devon region, only 17% used DCF against the 8% using this technique in the South Wessex Survey. These highly significant figures of 83% and 92% of the firms in the two samples using unsophisticated techniques, is an issue of some concern. In the South Wessex Survey the firms' attitudes tended to fall into two camps. Firms predominantly using the traditional methods believed that the quality of the investment decision was not influenced by the quality of the investment appraisal method, whilst firms employing modern techniques believed that the quality of the method could enhance the quality of the decision. However, it should be borne in mind that not all firms were able to distinguish one method from another, and sometimes confusions were evident. For example, several firms claimed no formal method of investment appraisal yet during discussions it was revealed that the payback method was in operation. Other companies employing modern techniques were by no means familiar with the mathematical problems inherent.

A point worth considering again is the degree of awareness of DCF displayed by the firms whilst not adopting the technique themselves. Of the 46 firms (92%) in the survey not using DCF, 36 companies (72%) claimed to be aware of the importance of DCF although no firm in the entire sample, as already indicated, was totally familiar with the technique. Several firms pointed out that since alternative projects were rarely taken into account alongside the capital item in question, then DCF was of limited relevance. But whilst this explanation might have been adequate in the circumstances described, it could not excuse the failure to consider other investment opportunities. Alternative projects were rarely considered alongside the project in question.

Moreover, of the 24 firms in the sample employing no formal method of investment appraisal, but basing their decisions on the necessity criterion, 20 of these firms (74%) were in the recession affected mechanical engineering industry. And although mechanical engineering firms were represented in the 4 firms actually employing DCF, in 3 of these cases the technique had been imposed on the firms by the parent company. Finally, in looking at the 14 firms claiming to be unaware of DCF, 10 (71%) were in mechanical engineering, One might be tempted to infer that many of this industry's problems were self-imposed.

It is quite possible that firms could be sub-optimising their investments and returns as a consequence of their inability, or even refusal, to employ more mathematical techniques. But to what extent did modern methods of investment appraisal actually contribute to investment optimality for the small firm? A review of the strengths and weaknesses of DCF is beyond the terms of reference of this work, except to state that DCF is regarded as a highly respectable method. Small firms must make themselves more aware of the real drawbacks of the methods they employ, although of course, this could be reasonably extended to those firms actually using DCF. A mere 8% of the South Wessex Survey firms used the technique, and no firm was really in tune with the problems of DCF and the possible solutions. Almost certainly, levels of investment and investment returns would be inconsistent with any prescribed goal of optimality.

Selection of the investment appraisal method

The firms that did actually use some method of investment appraisal were not always clear how, or why, the technique had been selected, or adopted, in the first instance. Practically no firm could claim to have been influenced by the literature on the subject. A notable defence of this position was the necessity criterion where on occasions the rate of return was only one factor among many to motivate investment decisions. But the conclusion that this actually removed the need for advanced DCF calculations, or even forecasts, was of more doubtful substance.

The South Wessex Survey firms were asked to recall how the method of appraisal, and the way in which cash flows were assessed, had been first introduced, or amended from time to time. Nearly half the sample (44%) explained that their investments had been appraised over the years by methods shrouded in tradition. Some of these firms stressed that whatever the drawbacks from employing obsolete techniques, these had proved adequate for the firm in question. It will be noted, again, that 48% did not employ a formal method of investment appraisal at all, relying on the necessity criterion as a major determinant of investment.

There were 24 firms admitting that their method of investment appraisal had either simply evolved, or its origin was historical. Of these 24 firms, 15 (62%) were in mechanical engineering. If this sector of industry was so prone to recessionary conditions it appeared that less reliance on tradition and more awareness of modern techniques, plus a willingness to change, was long overdue.

Cash flows

A further development of the investment appraisal method used, concerned the calculation of future cash flows at the appraisal stage. How were these estimates produced? How reliable were they?

Some 30% pointed out that the estimated net returns were based upon no formal method but on the necessity criterion assuming that all investment would simply pay for itself in time. A very small minority (2%) based their calculations on advice from their main supplier, and 14% used a miscellaneous savings approach. Some 10% felt that cash flows could not be estimated, 12% used pure guesswork and a remarkable 32% employed no method at all.

The problems of the mechanical engineering sector during recessionary conditions have been mentioned. There were 16 firms employing no apparent method of estimating future cash flows in their investment appraisals, and 11 of these (69%) were in the mechanical engineering area. Moreover, of the 15 firms relying on the necessity criterion. 9 (60%) were, again, mechanical engineers. The industry was quite able to identify its difficulties, but seemingly less able to correct them, for example, by more rigorous techniques.

Small firms' investment appraisal techniques, including cash flow estimation, could be observed to be lacking. Techniques can, within tolerable limits, be applied. Estimating is far more difficult.

Revision of the investment appraisal method

Largely as a consequence of the foregoing, attention was then focussed upon flexibility, a characteristic normally associated with the smaller firm. Had investment appraisal methods been subject to periodic revision, or improvement? Some 43 firms (86%) of the south Wessex sample admitted no revision at all, but 3 of these firms were already using DCF and improvement here had to be regarded as rather more difficult than the upgrading of payback.

Encouragingly, 8 firms (16%) had either upgraded their method to DCF, or were in the process of doing so. And 1 firm (2%) had even improved its DCF method. Since most of the firms that were either using DCF or were about to do so had been prompted by their parent companies, it gave rise to the important suggestion that if small firms had been similarly individually prompted by outside advisors, e.g. consultants, then investment appraisal might have significantly improved in this sector.

It was observed that 25 firms (50%) had not revised in any way their necessity criterion approach to investment appraisal. The mechanical engineering group complained of special difficulties arising from recessionary conditions. Firms in 'electronic engineering', it was argued by many, could always find markets in their developing sector, but there was little demand for machine tools from UK small firms, for example. Yet out of the 25 firms admitting total inflexibility of method, 16 (64%) were in mechanical engineering.

In general terms the small firms did not present an uplifting picture in respect of the selection of the investment appraisal method, the assessment of cash flows, and the flexibility of approach. The whole question of the use of other management techniques then arose. If small firms were not advanced in the use of modern DCF, did they compensate for this by the application of operations research in other areas? Unfortunately, this aspect could not be pursued in-depth, but some data were collected.

Management techniques

The respondents were asked to indicate the most important management technique employed including investment appraisal. The results were restricted to the choice of the one management technique considered to be indispensible for the firm's efficient operation. Even allowing for the fact that the nature of the industry and the type of production undertaken could influence this, it was striking that investment appraisal was accorded this priority by only 1 firm.

Budgeting in its widest sense appeared to be the most popular technique used (26% of the firms). If 'budgeting' was accepted as a legitimate technique then this still left 23 firms (46%) employing no major technique at all. This deficiency applied mainly to the smaller companies. If we reject budgeting as an acceptable technique then the statistic rises to 72%.

By way of comparison, some 20 years ago, the Engineering Training Board (1970) employed the Bristol Polytechnic Small Business Centre to survey a sample of engineering companies with up to 200 staff in four regions of England in their use of management techniques. Overall, it was found that some 50% of the firms in the sample employed no techniques. This compared with the 46% to 71% revealed in the South Wessex Survey. Investment appraisal did not even appear in the former survey whilst it scored only 2% usage in the latter.

The South Wessex Survey also showed that 9 firms (18%) admitted that certain techniques were applicable but these had not been employed to date, i.e. 1991. A mere 5 firms (10%) were using critical path analysis, work study, ratio analysis or value engineering.

Analysing the results further, out of the 23 firms employing no major technique, 16 (69%) were mechanical engineering companies. Additionally, out of the 9 firms conceding that certain techniques were applicable but not employed, 6 (67%) were, again, in this sector.

The degree of agreement with the Bristol study might or might not be significant. Further research was obviously needed in this area.

Management techniques then seemed to fall into two categories: those that were required for the normal production and financial monitoring, and those of a more advanced nature. The latter were not widely adopted and even basic forecasting, not to mention market research, was of a doubtful standard. A number of firms considered that forecasting was impossible, others believed that market research was far too expensive. But a few companies volunteered that although some management techniques could have been profitably applied they had never been introduced, and no sound reason for this was forthcoming. A minority of the sample felt that management techniques in general could mislead decisions.

It will be recalled from Chapter 2 that some firms felt that investment was occasionally imperative simply to adjust to a new situation, e.g. in order to remain in business. It was therefore not too surprising to have confirmed in Chapter 4 that firms did not feel the need for advanced techniques under such circumstances. In fact, 46% of the sample claimed that their method of investment appraisal had resulted from traditional usuage, and in most cases, had proved itself suitable for the nature of the firm and the industry in question.

Additionally, the point made that the rate of return was merely one factor among many which influenced investment could be misleading. Not all firms defined profit in the same way. Thus, if a firm said that investment was undertaken in order to speed up output, this was really another way of saying that investment was for profit. This was not in dispute. The issue under constant review was whether firms invested for optimum returns or not. The evidence suggested, again, that this was unlikely to be the case. Firms were not aiming for, or achieving, the optimum returns attainable via investment appraisal.

Factors taken into account in investment calculations

If it were assumed, and reasonably so, that certain factors, e.g. taxation, investment allowances, risk, inflation, etc., had to be included in the investment appraisal computation for accuracy, then the results from the south Wessex firms, and especially those that did employ a specific method of investment appraisal, were not encouraging.

The most popular factors taken into account appeared to be taxation, investment incentives and tax allowances if and when applicable, and inflation if at a high level. Some 24% of the sample (12 firms) acknowledged these, but strangely, depreciation was not listed. Moreover, only 8% felt the need to make adjustments for inflation. Many claimed that inflation was not predictable and thus it could not be meaningfully included. If the companies had been more DCF conscious, then an acceptable approach would have been to simply increase the discount factor by an amount appropriate to the level of inflation.

No firm felt that such items as risk, uncertainty, and likely obsolescence, could be mathematically catered for. A few of the firms that claimed to take inflation into account merely assumed it to be self-correcting by reduced returns being countered by increased prices in the market place. It was possible that some firms did make indirect allowance for risk, uncertainty, obsolescence, etc., but if they could not produce evidence of this in their examples, then these were ignored. It should be noted that risk refers to situations in which the outcome is not certain but where the probabilities of the alternative outcomes are known, or at least can be estimated. Uncertainty is present where the unknown outcomes cannot even be predicted in probabilistic terms, i.e. it refers to contingencies against which one cannot protect oneself on ordinary insurance principles.

A break-down of the industries involved showed that of the 22 firms (44%) not employing an investment appraisal method at all, 15 (68%) were in mechanical engineering. Since 67% of the firms in the sample were in this industry, this 68% is a result as adverse as some previously quoted ones. Of the 12 firms actually including factors in their calculations, 5 (42%) were specialist firms. Since 27% of the whole sample were such firms, then a 42% finding suggested that this recognition of factors was possibly the result of the demands of being in a specialist market where one-offs had to be individually calculated against competition, and equipment obtained in order to undertake the contract.

Bearing these points in mind 24% of the population made some kind of allowance for taxation, incentives, allowances, and inflation. The Taylor Nelson survey (1970) was of some relevance here. This work covered the pattern of industrial investment in the United Kingdom and included all sizes of firm. The results showed that of the 83 companies involved, 44 (53%) took taxation, allowances, etc., into account, whilst 35 (42%) did not. Four firms were recorded as undecided. Moreover, Taylor Nelson found that the companies expecting the higher returns were the ones that actually ignored the factors in question, and taxation allowances in particular. We have already observed in Chapters 2 and 3 that if governments were to raise profits directly in small firms in order to increase investment funds, then tax allowances would be of marginal influence only since they tended to be regarded as obscure, surrounded by bureaucracy, and obtained at too late a date. Taylor Nelson reported all this in 1970. It was not until the mid 1980's that government finally took notice, and not until the late 1980's that allowances were eventually phased out in favour of lower taxation.

The 53% taking factors into account from Taylor Nelson's larger firms compared reasonably with the 24% from the South Wessex Survey's much smaller units. The one question that remained was how were these factors catered for?

Undoubtedly the approach to method and the variables to be included inclined far more towards the trial and error than the mathematical. Whether or not some factors were self-correcting, self-cancelling, or simply non-measurable remained arguable, but in any event any or all of these would be no real substitute for rigour. Similarly although certain types of investment could overshadow the calculations and final accounts could automatically reflect net returns long term, this tended to simply confirm the rule of thumb attitude rather than defend it.

Investment appraisal examples

It was observed from a number of investment appraisal examples that the firms using the traditional techniques failed, in the main, to take full account of such factors as depreciation, taxation, inflation, obsolescence, returns after the break even point, opportunity cost, risk, uncertainty, projected demand for the product and alternative projects available. Moreover, the calculations ignored investment grants, and tax allowances, when available. In some instances, the necessity criterion obviously overshadowed the need for accurate cash flow and for a correct rate of return.

The firms employing discounted cash flow presented much better evaluations but even so some omitted several of the above factors, used excessively long time spans, provided obscure cash flows, were guilty of incorrect calculations and were unaware of the mathematical pitfalls of DCF generally.

Some firms in the south Wessex sample did realise that discounting had the important advantage of taking into account the time pattern of cash flows together with the cost of capital, and that other methods which did not do this could be considerd inferior for most purposes. And yet it has been shown, and stressed, that many capital expenditures were undertaken without discounting techniques being used. Two main reasons were put forward in defence of this practice. There were occasions when a reason of over-riding importance would make a precise evaluation of costs and returns by any method inappropriate. And although almost all projects were surrounded by a certain degree of uncertainty, some were more uncertain than others. In view of this, it seemed possible, but by no means certain, that firms could get near to the correct decision in the longer term without the application of mathematical techniques. In other words, they achieved survival returns from their sub-attitudes to investment appraisal. But were these survival returns the optimum? If firms failed to include all relevant data in their calculations and as a consequence rejected the project then they automatically reduced their attainable returns.

The conclusion had to be that whilst the sample firms could be described as survivors they nevertheless missed viable investment oportunities and effectively undermined even the returns obtained by inadequate investment appraisal.

Summary

In general terms the cost of capital was difficult to define but as far as the South Wessex Survey firms were concerned this had to be taken as that which individual companies either 'calculated' or simply believed that cost to be. The main investment appraisal methods used by the firms were the traditional techniques: 44% used either payback or rate of return, 8% employed discounted cash flow, and 48% used trial and error procedures or none at all. Of the 50 firms in the population 28% claimed to be unaware of discounted cash flow although no firm in the entire sample was totally familiar with the pitfalls of the technique. Firms that did actually use some method of investment appraisal were not always clear how or why the technique had been selected for use in the first instance, and 44% simply claimed their method to be of traditional origin. Practically no firm had been influenced by the literature on the subject. Advanced forecasting of cash flows was not in evidence and 32% used no method at all. Very few firms made attempts to assess cash flow on a calculated basis. A high 72% of the sample using traditional methods of appraisal, or none at all, admitted to no major amendments in system or policy. In general terms the very small companies did not present an encouraging picture of investment appraisal flexibility. Budgeting in its widest sense appeared to be the most popular management technique used but only one firm recorded investment appraisal as a major indispensable technique. The most significant factors taken into account in investment appraisal calculations were taxation, inflation, and investment incentives when available up to the late 1980's, but many other factors such as obsolescence, cost of capital, alternative projects, risk, and opportunity cost, were ignored. The firms employing the traditonal methods generally presented incomplete and inadequate appraisals. On the other hand, the companies using discounted cash flow produced much better evaluations but even so, were not immune from criticism. Overall, the investment appraisals and investment strategies practised were inconsistent with the goal of optimisation. And again, the mechanical engineering firms had to be singled out for special criticism in these respects.

References

British Institute of Management. (1972). 'The Needs of the Manager in the Small Company', *British Institute of Management Bristol Branch Discussion Paper No. 1*, June.

Hankinson, A.   (1979). ' Investment Appraisal in the Smaller
Firm',   *Management Accounting*, November, Vol. 57 (1),   p
37.

Taylor Nelson Investment Services.   (1970).   'The   Why and
How of Company   Investment', *The Director*,   November.

5 Profitability

Introduction

What pre-tax percentage return on investment was normally expected by the South Wessex Survey sample firms? Was this percentage rigid or variable? What minimum pre-tax percentage return was acceptable? Were there any specific reasons for failing to reach target rates of return on investment? Were expected rates of return invariably higher than actual? What could the firm do to make investment more efficient and effective? Could anything be done to raise investment returns on current investment? And had the firm ever employed outside expertise to assist with investment appraisal and investment decision making generally? Despite the problems of data collection and interpretation, an examination of these areas was hoped to throw some light upon investment performances.

Target rate of return on investment

Although profit was unquestionably of major concern to small

firms, the evidence was not strong that managerial estimates
of the relationship between marginal cost and marginal
revenue actually formed the basis for price selection.
Rather, pricing policies indicated a widespread reliance
upon target return pricing methods. In the South Wessex
Survey the desired profit target was, for example, stated as
a profit on sales of 5%, a profit return equal to 10% on
total assets, a profit return equal to 15% of net worth
(stockholders' equity), a profit return equal to 20% on net
worth plus long term debt, or as simply a specific pounds
sterling figure. The size of the profit target tended to
hinge upon such considerations as industry custom,
competitive pressures, what managers believed to be a fair
or reasonable return, a desire to equal or better the firm's
recent profit performance, a desire to stabilise industry
prices, whether the firm's product was new or established,
and the firm's related goals of sales, market share and
growth. Additionally, specific profit targets tended to
differ among industries and firms reflecting differing
degress of competition and differing priorities among
alternative goals.
 The mechanics of target pricing might be geared towards
pricing to obtain a desired return on sales, i.e. cost plus
pricing, or pricing to achieve a target return on
investment. In practice, both pricing to achieve a target
return on investment, and cost plus pricing offered
relatively simple and expedient methods of price
determination which had a demonstrated ability to yield
adequate, fair, or reasonable profits. Once the target
price had been chosen, the usual procedure of the south
Wessex firms was to stick by the price and sell whatever
amounts of output that short run demand conditions
permitted. The target return price was, therefore, a stable
price. However, target return pricing did have the effect
of making profits quite variable, although the 1980-1991
periodic recessionary conditions could not be overlooked in
this respect. But in any event, on a year to year basis,
actual profits turned out to be either higher or lower than
the target profit rate. One question indeed was whether
profits tended to be mainly lower than the target, or higher
 It follows that target return pricing was not a strategy
for maximising profits. Actually, the concept of rigid
target return pricing exemplified a behavioural pattern
closely approximating to surviving. The target rate of
return, according to the south Wessex firms, tended to be
based upon managerial concepts of what was an equitable,
reasonable, or survival, rate of return given the degrees of
risk and uncertainty involved.
 The target rate of return on net assets and the mark-up on
costs are related by MU = Target X Net Assets / Sales. But

the south Wessex firms that, in the main, failed to reach their targets, could hardly have done otherwise with the mark-ups employed. In short, far too many firms were not aware of the above relationship.

Attention may now be turned towards the extent the south Wessex firms employed rates of return on investment. The more rigid the targets and the less likely would be the achievement of profit optimality.

Expected rate of return on investment

Some twenty years ago the Taylor Nelson Survey (1970) researched the rate of return on investment required by their sample of U.K. companies. Applying a standard which excluded any special risk factors, among the directors who gave a positive reply, over half opted for a yield of between 15%-19%, or 5 to 6 years payback. But there was an interesting spread of expectations. A small though significant group expected yields of under 14%, whilst a second perhaps more optimistic category, expected returns above 20%, i.e. a payback on the investment in 4 years or fewer. This more optimistic category in the Taylor Nelson sample included relatively few large companies and was made up of mainly small and medium sized concerns.

However, with regard to the South Wessex Survey firms' expected pre-tax percentage returns on investment, these could only be estimated since, for example, several firms adopted different targets for different projects. But one factor was confirmed. Firms using the payback or rate of return methods, i.e. some 44% of the sample, tended to accept that actual returns need not necessarily coincide with the original target. Uncertainty in the market, falling demand, excess capacity, short time working, inflation during the 1988-1991 period, excessive interest rates, foreign competition and general uncertainty were some of the responses given for the likely shortfalls.

Another problem, already indicated, was that not all firms laid down a specific payback or rate of return target in that some investment would be undertaken irrespective of the return. Thus, as estimating a return was not easy, firms were asked to quote the expected rate of return necessary for the project in question to proceed. Comparison with Taylor Nelson (1970) revealed a decided uplift in expectations in favour of the south Wessex firms.

It would probably surprise few owners to learn that with late 1980's and early 1990's inflation, for example, running at up to 9% at one point a large number of companies expected a higher rate of return from projects compared with

a few years ago. Perhaps other managing directors would be
more surprised to read that several firms required only the
same return as a few years ago. But it must be stated that
companies expecting no more than the same yield may well
have reflected their estimate of reality rather than what
owners would have wished to realise. Indeed a diversion
from the Taylor Nelson findings was the 30% of the South
Wessex Survey firms resignedly looked to the market to
produce a rate of return which then in retrospect served as
the target. This was probably explained by the conditions
of 1989, 1990 and 1991 such as high interest rates and
rising inflation, as opposed to the late 1970's.
  The evidence suggested that because of higher costs of
money and rising wage bills alone, firms might well have
been forced to look for higher yields on their capital
investments. It is also important to remember that these
required rates of return would not necessarily bring in the
same amount of profit as a year ago. In fact, much of the
evidence suggested that even while requiring higher returns
from their capital spending, small companies had faced
steadily falling or stable profits over recent years.
  The evidence would appear, at first glance, to support the
flexible target argument. However, the overall picture
should be viewed cautiously since it does not represent the
behaviour of each individual unit. Many firms in the sample
did employ a fixed rate of return or payback in the short,
medium and even longer term, but others adopted different
targets depending on the area of operations, the item in
question, the size of the project, the nature of the
investment, the rate of inflation, the profit margin
required, the historical return on capital ratio, losses
sustained at the time, market or political uncertainty and
the return being greater than 0%. Some companies actually
waived the rate of return on certain capital items, others
quoted no calculations at all, whilst a few claimed only to
invest if they could pay cash. Moreover, it was not
impossible on one-off jobs for the expected rate of return
to be below 0% if a contract were likely to follow. Here
the firm would probably have accepted the prototype first,
and then set about acquiring suitable machinery to do the
work.
  The main point to emerge on this issue was that despite the
appearance of flexibility, the targets once set, tended to
prevail in the majority of cases, e.g. X% on buildings, Y%
on machinery, and Z% on vital investment. Thus, the
inference was that, in the main, targeting was somewhat
rigid for individual firms producing survival returns on
investment at best. And it must be remembered that 30% of
the sample simply allowed the market to produce the target,
a non-aspirational policy that can only be equated with

survival.

Minimum target rate of return

Despite the finding that targeting tended to be somewhat
rigid, it could not be overlooked that in certain cases a
minimum rate of return would be acceptable. Estimating this
minimum had to be considered in the light of the various
influences affecting current and expected rates of return in
general such as market conditions, political climate,
overseas developments including the EEC and the necessity
criterion. The findings revealed that whilst some 26% of
the sample expected a 20% rate of return or over, only 2
firms would expect a minimum rate return over 20%. In fact
almost half of the firms that did lay down a target claimed
they would, from experience, reluctantly have to settle for
a rate between 0% and 10% only. Of the firms relaxing their
targets the most prevalent were in the 0-24 employee group.
The extent of this lowering of sights could have indicated
the lack of effectiveness in the firms' abilities to meet
the targets laid down, the effect of economic uncertainty in
the past (1980 up to 1991), or a combination of both. In
view of the evidence already presented the former point
could not be dismissed lightly. For example, when actual
rates of return on net assets were examined there was
generally an even poorer performance. Whilst several firms
had exceeded their expectations, many had not reached their
targets, others had failed to achieve the minimum, and some
had sustained losses in the ten year period under review.
If investment optimisation were to occur one might
reasonably expect the target rate of return to be variable,
but we have already seen some evidence of rigidity. Whilst
minimum target rates could range from 0% upwards, this
flexibility did not necessarily apply to vertical
investment, i.e. real increases in capital stocks.
Generally, replacement items were regarded as crucial, along
with investment for health and safety, and any return
greater than 0% appeared to be acceptable. On the other
hand, some firms felt that the minimum target depended on
the goals of the company at the time, several regarded the
minimum as that actually borne by the market in the previous
or current period, whilst others equated the lower limit
with trade investment returns, bank deposit interest and the
rate of inflation. Very few firms held that any percentage
return over the cost of borrowing would be acceptable on
vertical projects, but the majority were quite prepared to
exercise some flexibility on non-vertical investment. It
was apparent that if the firms had extended

the latter policy to the former, and provided that the yield had exceeded the discount rate, then investment optimisation might have been rather more pursuable.

Reasons for failing to reach expected rate of return

The major reasons for the failure to reach expected rates of return appeared to be external such as industry trade cycling, inflation, base rates, competition and general recessionary conditions.   It was interesting to note that only 2 firms consistently blamed the government for their disappointing results.   A further 6 firms felt that governments had been at least partially responsible.   Many of the reasons given were individual, but most firms, i.e. 62%, considered that the 'external situation' was the principal factor that had caused actual returns to be but a fraction of those expected or required.   However, most significant of all was that only 16% (8 firms) admitted the possibility that their inadequate investment strategies, general inexpertise and suspect mathematical appraisals could have given rise to financial performances being well below those reasonably attainable.

Although a sub-sample of 8 firms admitting their own inadequacies was far too small to be meaningful it was notable that 75% of this small group were in electrical engineering, and only 25% in mechanical engineering.   The latter group has been already been exposed in several tests of investment behaviour undertaken in this work.   It was the more successful electrical engineering group that was more prepared to admit to those managerial deficiencies most likely to impair investment profitability.

Since targeting was basically a ratio approach, i.e. profit as a percentage of net assets, and since the firms in question appeared to get this ratio wrong more often than right, could this have been partly responsible for sub-standard performances? One crucial factor in the failure of small businesses over the years was the lack of adequate investment.   In the South Wessex Survey no firm in the entire sample gave this as a possible reason for failing to reach targets set by the firms themselves.

Improvement of investment performance

Given periodic adverse business conditions signs of recovery were always in the offing and normally firms sensing that a recession had bottomed out would be poised to increase capital spending in order to cope with an increased future demand. Unfortunately, the south Wessex firms' investment strategies did not necessarily include this fundamental principle. Moreover, even when investment had actually occurred, returns had not always achieved the target set. Could the firms themselves suggest what might be done to make investment more effective and to raise investment returns?

Only 14% of the sample 50 firms had considered the issues sufficiently to reach the conclusion that a more positive investment strategy, including investment appraisal, was required, and the majority of these were electrical engineering firms. An even more remarkable feature was the 58% that believed no action could be taken to raise performance since their activities were constrained by such factors as external market forces. A futher item of interest was that firms having agreed that certain measures were needed to improve investment decisions and returns, then stated that the likelihood of these actions actually being carried out was remote. Despite the wide range of suggestions put forward, there was apparently no guarantee that the firms in question would implement them.

In general terms it appeared from the data collected that there were three basic rules to be followed in order that investment performance might be improved: increase the rate of investment whether it involved borrowing or not; use existing capital equipment far more efficiently and intensively; and choose new investment far more carefully with the help of approved investment appraisal techniques. Unfortunately these rules were not being employed by the sample firms.

Management consultancy

When expected and actual rates of return were compared there were disappointments. In other words, and as already indicated, whilst several firms had exceeded their expectations, others had not reached their targets. Some of these had failed to achieve even the minimum acceptable rate of return, and a minority had actually sustained losses.

The reasons given by 62% of the firms for these adverse results were claimed to be 'external factors' such as inflation, competition, the periodic recessions of the 1980's and early 1990's, unpredictable government policy, large firms failing to pay their bills on time, etc. A further 22% identified the causes as 'managerial' including forecasting, excess capacity, under pricing, lack of funds, too few managerial techniques employed, labour difficulties and so on. But a significant pointer was that only 16% actually expressed doubts about their own investment expertise. A remarkable 58% of the sample felt that no action could be taken to raise performance appreciably since the external factors constraining the firm were believed to be uncontrollable. But even the 14% that favoured a positive investment strategy and more rigorous investment appraisal, once again, could not guarantee that such action would be implemented. More than suspecting that the reason for this might be lack of even basic managerial ability in the investment field, the South Wessex Survey interviewees were asked if their firms had ever employed management consultants to assist with investment appraisal and investment decision making.

Only 4% of the 50 firm sample had resorted to outside expertise specifically for occasional investment purposes. A further 24% felt that external assistance might be useful and would consider it should the occasion demand. But 72% had neither employed not had considered employing outside advice for investment reasons. An interesting feature was that although many firms had no experience of consultants they, nevertheless, considered them to be over rated, expensive, inventors of problems and representative of external interference and control. Firms felt that their own experiences and abilities were more likely to solve problems than any outside factor, and out of the full sample 17 firms (34%) put this point strongly. Some 13 companies (26%) regarded the advice from banks, auditors, accountants, the Engineering Industries Association and parent companies as extensions of their own expertise rather than direct external consultancy.

Effectively, no firm in the sample had employed investment consultants significantly, and the majority had employed no outside assistance at all. Yet many interviewees felt able to comment adversely on the value of consultancy generally. It was significant that the firms actually using consultants were well satisfied with their efforts.

Respondents considered that management consultants tended not to devote much attention to the very small firm anyway. The management consultancy profession had grown rapidly and had maintained a high level of resource employment by homing in on the larger firms. There was little incentive for the profession to venture into the unproven and difficult area of consultancy for the firm with up to 10 employees. Fundamentally, there were at least two problems. First, the small firm consultancy operation was not necessarily more simple than advising a large firm, and in some ways more difficult. And second, the pronounced sales resistance of the typical small firm required an equally strong marketing effort which most consultants would not be prepared to make.

It appeared that consultants that had tried consultancy in the smaller firm claimed that the most common reason for the rejection of their services was the cost. Firms maintained that fees were excessive or that they were simply unable to meet whatever fees were quoted. High cost was very often advanced as a respectable ground for refusal by small business owners whose real objections to consultancy were unwillingness to disturb a comfortable routine and the fear that close inspection would reveal their own inadequacies. There was also a strong element of prejudice against outside interference based on the common idea that expertise in how to run a business was best gained, and most profitably exercised, by actually running one. The prejudiced attitude towards management consultants among the firms was unfortunate since most businessmen would probably have gained from an objective and skilled appraisal of their performances, and from the application of well tried methods to their problems.

To what extent were the firms justified in taking this stance? Two studies, one from 1968-1969 and the other undertaken in 1988-1991, might help to answer the question.

In June 1968 the then Board of Trade announced a scheme, reported by Jones (1974), to encourage the wider use of consultancy by small firms. It aimed at firms with between 25 and 500 staff although it was made clear that these were not rigid limits. Any use of consultants had to be linked to the expectation of increasing the efficiency of the undertaking. In practice 'efficiency' was given a wide definition. When consultants were used in this way and provided prior approval had been obtained, the Board of Trade would pay half the consultants' fees, including expenses, up to a maximum of £5000. The scheme closed on 28 February 1969 in that no further applications for grants were accepted after that date. However, the assignments financed under the scheme were only finalised during 1972.

The majority of the firms that took part (166 out of 227) were either private limited companies or subsidiaries of such companies. A further 45 firms were public limited companies or subsidiaries of such concerns. And 133 out of the 227 were firms with fewer than 200 employees. Moreover, manufacturing units had more assignments on average than did the other firms.

A breakdown of the total cost of the assignments revealed that 40% cost no more than £2000, whilst 60% cost no more than £3000. Of the assignments chosen finance and administration were dominant, but the extent of investment in this area was unfortunately not declared.

A small number of the firms had used consultants before but those firms not having done so were asked whether there was a specific reason for this. The response given most often was that they had never felt the need to use consultants. In fact this reason was offered in about 60% of the cases whilst in another 18% the firms felt that consultants were too expensive. The other 22% of the reasons given were a mixed group and included such items as opposition within the firm, put off by experiences of other firms, firms not in existence for long enough and so on. It should be noted that these were also typical responses by the South Wessex Survey firms.

The firms using the scheme were asked whether they were satisfied with the consultants who had carried out the assignments in question. In 185 out of the 258 assignments the firms were satisfied. In 61 cases they were partially satisfied, and in 12 cases only they were dissatisfied. Thus, in a mere 4.6% instances the consultancy did not meet the firms' expectations.

In order to check how much the firms had been encouraged to use consultants they were asked if they would use consultants again. In 65 cases out of the 227 consultants had already been used a second time. Where firms had not used consultants since the scheme ended, 149 said they would, and only 10 said they would not, with the remaining 3 undecided. In other words, a remarkable 93% of the group claimed that consultancy had been employed, or would be employed again.

To assess the attitudes of the firms to the consultants' recommendations they were asked how many of the suggestions had been adopted. In 200 of the 258 assignments (78%) over half had been adopted whilst in only 11 assignments none had been implemented. On this measure only 11 could be regarded as complete failures whilst 200 were at least reasonably successful.

Often in consultants' reports an estimate of average savings or benefits likely to result from the adoption of their recommendations will be made. In 90 assignments some assessment was given of the benefits to the firm, e.g. £16000 in the first year, and just over £15000 in subsequent years. The total consultants' fees for these 90 assignments were just over £434,000 giving an average of £4882. Thus, if the consultants' recommendations had been adopted and the savings and benefits achieved there would have been a quantifiable non-discounted return of some 330% on the total consultants' fees for the assignments in the first year of their adoption. In actuality, the firms themselves claimed that the benefits were about two thirds of this return. This still meant, of course, that on average, in the early 1970's, the total fees were recouped well within the first year.

In summary, 95% of the firms in the Department of Industry sample were either satisfied or partially satisfied with the consultants employed; 93% claimed that they had already used, or would use, consultants again; 78% of the assignments carried out were regarded as reasonably successful by the firms; and the net benefits were estimated by the firms themselves to be over 200% in the first year alone.

A second investigation, undertaken by Hankinson, covered the period 1988-1991 in the same region as the South Wessex Survey. This study of 17 engineering firms with up to 100 staff and with direct experience of consultants, but not part of the south Wessex sample, also proved to be an interesting contrast. The consultancies covered a wide range of activities both in the technical and managerial fields. When asked whether they were satisfied with the consultants who carried out the assignments nearly 70% (12 firms) were well satisfied. In 3 other cases out of the 17 there was partial satisfaction with some of the work carried out. And in only 2 firms was there general dissatisfaction. Would the firms use consultants again? All 17 claimed that they would, including the firms with some reservations.

To assess the attitude of the firms to the consultants' recommendations they were asked how many of the suggestions made by the consultants had been adopted. In 15 firms well over half had been applied, whilst in only 2 firms none been implemented.

Regarding the consultants' estimates of the savings likely to result from their recommendations, the firms claimed that on average whatever the consultants' stated savings or benefits were, the total fees were recouped mainly in the first or second year of operation.

Thus, in summarising a rather complex analysis, 88% of the 17 firm sample were either satisfied or partially satisfied with the consultants employed. All 17 firms reported that they would use consultants again, or they had already contacted consultants with further assignments.

In view of the findings of these two studies it must be reasonable to conclude that the South Wessex Survey firms' reservations about consultancy were probably very much over-stated and they might well have benefited from the outside expertise they chose to reject. In short, investment optimality in particular could well have been pursued rather more purposefully with the help of consultancy than without it.

Summary

The policy of rigid target return pricing, which exemplified a behavioural pattern closely approximating to survival, was

generally employed by the south Wessex firms. The minimum
acceptable rate of return tended to be determined by
specific circumstances or events, and any apparent
flexibility was directed more towards horizontal rather than
vertical investment. The severe difficulties of measuring
firms' performances were recognised but since many of the
south Wessex firms expressed their profitability in terms of
a rate of return on net assets, this criterion was adopted.
Whilst several firms had exceeded their targets, a majority
had not reached their expectations, and some of these had
failed to achieve even the minimum rate of return, with a
few sustaining losses at least in the short run. The major
reason given for failing to reach expected rates of return
was 'uncontrollable external factors'. Only a minority of
the firms considered that their own inadequate investment
strategies, expertise and appraisals might have caused
financial performance to be below optimum. Only a minority
felt that a more positive investment strategy was required,
and many believed that no action could be taken to raise
performance owing to outside constraints. No firm could
guarantee that any suggestions put forward to improve
returns would in fact be implemented. A highly significant
percentage of the firms had neither employed, nor had
considered employing, outside expertise, believing
consultants to be unnecessary, over-rated, expensive,
inventors of problems, disruptive and representative of
external interference. Given the findings of two studies of
consultancy some twenty years apart it appeared that the
South Wessex Survey firms' strong reservations about
consultancy were very much overstated and outside expertise
could well have aided the pursuit of investment optimality.

References

Jones, C. D. (1974). 'Consultancy in the Smaller Firm',
Department of Industry, London,

Taylor Nelson Investment Services. (1970). 'The Why and How
of Company Investment', *The Director*, November.

6 Pricing

Introduction

How was price actually calculated for routine batches and
one-off jobs? Which factors merely influenced price? What
percentage profit margin was normally added? Was this mark-
up rigid or variable? What minimum percentage profit margin
would be acceptable? How was price adjusted for inflation?
How cost conscious were the sample firms? What would be the
effect on sales of marginal increases in price? How
flexible were small firms? What were their overall
investment strategies with particular reference to pricing?
What could small firms do to make pricing more effective?
To what extent had the economic climate influenced pricing
decisions? Had the firms ever employed management
consultants to assist with pricing policy or decisions? And
what could, or should, the government do to make pricing
decisions easier for small firms? Chapter 6 attempts to
answer these questions.

Pricing studies

The literature on pricing behaviour is somewhat inconsistent. Hall and Hitch (1939) found that firms were vague about the mechanics of marginalism and relied instead upon full cost pricing. These findings were largely paralleled by Sweezy (1939). Earley (1956), however, suggested that marginalism was strongly implanted in pricing behaviour. Hague (1959) reported that firms were less interested in profit maximisation than in secure incomes. Firms based price upon total cost not unlike the Hall and Hitch conception. Skinner (1970) concluded that cost plus percentage pricing was very much influenced by competition and demand. And firms making the distinction between fixed costs and variable costs were, in essence, employing marginalism. But Sizer (1971) rejected Skinner's interpretation of the latter. Silbertson (1970) felt that full cost pricing was well established but there were many marginalist and behavioural qualifications. Sowter, Gabor and Granger (1971) conducted tests to show that price was a crucial element in explaining consumer behaviour. There was a strong relationship between sales and price. Udell (1966) had earlier concluded that business management did not agree with the economic views of the importance of pricing as one half of his respondents had not selected pricing as one of the five most important policy areas in the firm's marketing success. Sowter (1973) using buyer-response curves, found that price acted as an indicator of quality. Harcourt and Kenyon (1976), in examining larger firms, held that the size of the mark-up and the level of planned investment were related, givien expectations about future demand. The relevance of the theory to the smaller firm was open to some doubt as far as the South Wessex Survey firms were concerned. Gabor (1977) reported that until recently (up to 1977) pricing had indeed been ruled by hit or miss instinct, but there was now more objective and systematic. On the other hand, Stone (1980) stated that the main problem in pricing were not problems of principle but empirical ones in that pricing was based upon information, and information collection was invariably of doubtful quality. Not surprisingly, contributors have felt uncertain about the various pricing studies available. And material in relation to regional real world small firm pricing remains lacking. Consequently, the questions posed in the introduction would appear to assume an even greater importance than might first be hypothesised.

Determinants and influences

A firm pursuing its objectives must demonstrate its ability
to assess correctly the many parameters of the market in
which it belongs. Particularly the firm has to determine
the price which will optimise its profits or sales. Both
these depend upon the responses of the market to the price
set in the first instance. However, it is not necessarily
true to state that in practice its pricing policy is a
matter of the utmost concern to a firm. The Udell study
(1966) supported this. Moreover, the aiming for certain
obkectives does demand that prices be fixed according to
some formula which obviates management discretionary pricing
policies.

There are many situations in which pricing decisions
require considerable skill and expertise and any firm that
seeks to optimise returns must constantly vary prices in
line with changes in demand. Not least, careful pricing
almost certainly was of some relevance for small firm
survival during 1980-1991. Assuming that output levels were
pre-determined a firm intent on optimisation would
presumably aim for the highest possible price at that
production level. Incidentally, the assumption of rigid
output levels is well founded as far as the South Wessex
Survey is concerned and is demonstrated in Chapter 7. Few
firms systematically amended production levels in order to
optimise profits. If it could be shown that firms did not
employ flexible pricing at all, i.e. not charging the
optimum price in response to market conditions, rivalry,
discount opportunities, negotiation, targeting, prestige
customers, hire versus sales, price lining, quality and
technology, and above all, contribiution potential, then
inadequate pricing would clearly be the case.

Consequently, how did the south Wessex firms actually
calculate price? Which factors merely influenced price?
There are, in fact, several cost plus theories but they
have, in the main, a common base. Firms in the South Wessex
Survey using this method simply set price by estimating
production costs and adding on a percentage mark-up for
profit. Whilst it was true that all firms were basically
cost conscious and made this the essence of price
calculation, only 18% of the sample with the larger firms
predominating claimed that non-cost pricing was practised.
Costs had to be covered in the first instance but the
ultimate selling price would be determined by what the
market would bear at the output level in question, or the
price set by competitors.

The impact of rival prices was surprisingly not strong.
Competition was certainly acknowledged but only by 4 firms.
Rarely did a rival price actually determine the price for

the firm itself. This was not to say that firms were not influenced by external factors. It will be remembered that firms often blamed 'external factors' for various problems. Under certain conditions, e.g. falling demand, firms would be affected by market conditions. The issue under consideration here was determination of price rather than price influences.

The most striking characteristic of the findings was the significant majority that firmly based price on cost. Some 82% set price by estimating full costs and adding their arbitrary percentage mark-ups in the Hall and Hitch (1939), Sweezy (1939) and Hague (1959) traditions. The Silbertson (1970) view of C+% was also confirmed but there was little evidence of price being determined by 'marginalist and behavioural' qualifications or by the 'strong marginalism' forwarded by Earley (1956). And the 'rivalry and demand' determinants as suggested by Skinner (1970) were somewhat weak. Although 82% used full cost pricing it should be noted that firms identified specific foundations of price. Labour, materials, overheads and targeting were some examples. A surprising omission was expected costs. Despite a tolerable inflation rate throughout the 1980's, interviewees constantly complained of rising costs of production, but it seemed that in the light of the other issues, expected costs were rated low as a price determinant.

The evidence did tend to support the various contributors who had claimed that pricing was dominated by the C+% method. Even where opportunities existed for more flexible pricing, e.g. on one-off jobs, these openings were largely ignored. Sometimes different margins were applied to different products. However, whether these mark-ups were fixed or flexible, and the latter was mainly the case, the end result was short run price rigidity in the main. It could well be argued that price leadership by certain large firms reduced many of the small firms in question to price takers, but even so, some of these firms at least, could have employed a little more flexibility in their pricing. Some firms were heavily entrenched in price conservatism, e.g. stable prices irrespective of market trends, and as in the Udell (1966) study they clearly felt that pricing was not necessarily a top priority for successful operation. In any event, since internal information on costs, market research, demand, etc., were rather inadequate, firms found it virtually impossible to apply profit optimising pricing rules. Additionally, the impression was that surprisingly few firms in the survey considered that profits could be raised significantly simply by adopting flexible pricing. Some doubted if flexibility could be implemented at all. At best, sub-optimum profit could only be expected. It seemed remarkable that the majority of firms should opt for the cost plus percentage method of pricing when its limitations were obvious.

The cost plus method effectively ignored market conditions and profits or sales could be lost. Cost plus assumed accurate calculations of cost and this was almost certainly not the case for the majority of the sample firms. The price fixed by cost plus was far too rigid and very rapidly became out of date in relation, for example, to rival pricing. If prices were rigid during periods of high inflation the firms found it even more difficult to make the highest level of profit reasonably attainable. Inflationary conditions required prices to be raised by small amounts and often. Delayed price adjustments by the firms prevented them from reaching their target rates of return.

On the other hand, however, supporters of cost plus claimed that the method did produce a fair price which many businessmen favoured. It was simple to understand and this appealed to both manufacturer and customer. Some respondents argued that cost plus pricing could produce optimum profits over the longer term by trial and error means. In other words, if the price were adjusted occasionally in order to rectify shortfalls, then target profit could well be reached over time. Other firms felt that cost plus did tend to lead to an element of market confidence if prices were fairly stable.

The South Wessex Survey data gave the clear impression that pricing tended to be rigid. Indeed, several firms claimed that price stability was a specific policy of the company. Only 18% of the sample were engaged in what might be described as flexible pricing on normal production. But did this mean that the majority of the firms never practised market pricing? When interviewees were asked specifically about price influences, if applicable, there appeared to be more flexibility than one might have supposed.

It was revealed that only 28% of the sample still persisted with the notion that full costs not only determined but also influenced pricing. It will be recalled that in terms of price determinants only 82% originally claimed that there was little alternative to cost plus pricing. Now, other factors were brought into consideration. These other factors fell into two categories: internal and external. The former included technical problems on the workshop floor, varying work loads and overheads. The latter comprised rivalry, government intervention, market trends, international issues, inflation and recessionary economic conditions. In short, whilst 28% still opted for full costs as major influences, 14% now turned to internal non-cost plus factors. And 58% acknowledged that external considerations were more important. This move away from full cost must be regarded as significant and represenatative of a more flexible approach to pricing albeit from a low base.

It is interesting that commentators tend not to make the distinction between price determinants and influences, and this might go some way towards explaining the occasional conflict in the literature.

In the South Wessex Survey then cost plus pricing dominated the fixing of price in the short run, but over the longer term price might be adjusted in response to changing conditions not necessarily connected with costs. Nevertheless, even if some firms did respond occasionally to changes in demand and profitability shortfalls by amending price, they certainly did not do this in a conscious profit optimising manner. And even the price initiators, e.g. those pricing one-off production items, appeared to have the policy forced upon them by events.

The vital question was whether firms wished to optimise profits or not? If the former were the case, and one must assume that it was since the firms did set themselves targets, then the inflexible pricing practised might be identified as one further reason why levels of profit were below those reasonably attainable for most of the firms that preferred to blame the occasional recessionary conditions during 1980 to 1991. It was true that several interviewees believed that if they, like their rivals, had adhered to a simple pricing rule based upon costs, they would in the longer term maximise their profits. The underlying rationale here was that this would avoid the possibility of price wars and the like, and thus, eliminate an important source of uncertainty surrounding the firm's future actions. As the long run was an amorphous concept at best, one could not determine empirically whether the above was correct or not. Therefore, it was probably reasonable to state that whilst pricing based upon costs would certainly not lead to maximum or even optimium profits, it was nevertheless, analogous to the satisficing behaviour described by Simon (1959) (1962) giving rise to satisficing profits but no more.

One-off pricing

Of the 16 one-off production firms in the sample only 2 were using a rigid cost plus percentage approach. A further 8 adopted the basic cost plus method but employed a far more flexible attitude to pricing. For example, they subjected price to the market, the contract to tender or engaging in negotiations. The remaining 6 firms preferred a non-cost plus policy and displayed marked price flexibility in their dealings. Thus, some 88% of the specialist firms could be identified as employers of varying degrees of price flexibility.

Taking the 50 firm sample as a whole 14 firms did not undertake one-off jobs. The 36 firms that were able to perform one-off functions consisted of all three categories of production capability, i.e. specialist, standardiser and repeater. Some companies in this 36 firm group used rigid cost plus pricing for both routine and one-off operations. There were 8 of these firms. Another group in this 36 sub-sample employed flexible pricing for both routine and one-off contracts. There were 6 of these firms. But the significant group was the 22 firms that adopted rigid cost plus pricing for routine production and flexible pricing for one-offs.

It appeared that flexible pricing was by no means impracticable, at least on one-off contracts and, no doubt, profit resulted. No firm claimed that one-offs were consistently unprofitable. This was not meant to declare, of course, that flexible pricing guaranteed optimum profit, although the survey findings did hint at this possibility over rigid approaches to pricing. What was demonstrated was that flexibility was possible, was practised, and was no doubt successful, but almost entirely on one-off activities.

What emerged from this examination of price determinants might be effectively summarised by Haynes (1962). Haynes researched 88 small firms in the manufacturing, retailing and service sectors employing for the most part fewer than 200 employees. His conclusions which corresponded favourably with the observations made in respect of the South Wessex Survey were as follows. Prices were more often based upon costs rather than upon demand. Mark-up pricing was common. Mark-ups were set at different levels for different products. Price leadership by large firms made some small firms price followers. And information for the application of economic market pricing was poor.

Two arguments among others have been forwarded as the main reasons for the widespread use of cost plus pricing. One was that firms were satisficers not maximisers. Associated with this argument was the belief that some firms genuinely wanted only a fair or just rate of profit, a point already made above.

The second argument was that in an uncertain world firms just could not estimate all the permutations of all the variables that should be taken into account in order to derive the optimum price. The possible permutations were numerous and even simple problems could turn out to be complex. The south Wessex firms saw cost plus percentage pricing as the best solution in a complicated and unpredictable business world. The achievement of, long run optimum profit was very much dependent on the ability of managing directors to overcome volatile conditions in the market.

Mark-ups

Closely linked to cost plus pricing is pricing to achieve a target rate of return on investment. In order to implement targeting firms in setting out to achieve the target should calculate the approximate mark-up on full costs according to the formula:

% mark-up to	Target		Net Assets
achieve target =	rate	X	————
rate of return	of		
on net assets	return		Sales

There was some evidence of the sample firms adopting target rates of return on net assets as a yardstick of success. Targeting as an objective appeared to be fairly well established. But it should be noted that many of the firms invariably failed to reach these targets. If the % mark-up was set below that determined by the formula then targets would not be reached. Even if the mark-ups were initially correct but firms did not adjust price in response to changing conditions, then the mark-up would soon become insufficient to achieve the target. It must be stated at this point that very few of the south Wessex firms actually employed the formula.

The analysis of the mark-ups of the firms was difficult both because of the nature of financial records and because of conceptual difficulties of definition and actual measurement. As a result of varying accounting practices the size of one firm's recorded mark-up might differ from others in the same line of business and situation. There might be arbitrary differences in mark-up definition for ranges of products, differences in identifying priority cost areas and in the allocation of expenses incurred during a particular year which related to activities of other years. In a small firm owned by a family or closely knit group of people additional problems might exist which add to the difficulty of inter-firm comparison. More often than not the mark-up figure was the information which firms were most reluctant to give. It might well be for tax reasons or because of fear of competition or it might be inaccurate because of a lack of correct information on the part of the firm's management. Nevertheless, the overall impression of sub-optimum returns emerged strongly.

Pricing and inflation

Inflation might be regarded as a condition where the volume of purchasing power was persistently running ahead of the output of goods and services available to consumers and producers with the result that there was a persistent tendency for prices and wages to rise.

If prices were rising business activity would be stimulated. Production would be carried on in anticipation of demand and as all costs would not increase immediately prices began to rise, so profit margins would be greater than expected. There was therefore, less risk to the producer who would increase his output as much as possible, for as long as rising costs lagged behind rising prices his profits would be greater than before.

On the other hand, if prices were falling profit margins would be smaller than was expected when production was undertaken. A severe fall in prices might result in a loss, for costs of production would not fall proportionately with commodity prices, wages being especially difficult to adjust. To producers the outlook would appear uncertain and they would tend to restrict their output. If it were desired to maintain a high level of production gently rising prices were to be preferred than falling ones.

If inflation were severe and there was evidence of world recession then manufacturers would not be prepared to to produce goods for which there might not be an eventual demand. Unemployment might then result compounding the recession at home. Thus, rapidly rising prices could actually cause production to fall.

Bearing all this in mind how did the south Wessex firms adjust prices for inflation?

With inflation in single figures only 5 firms had the clear policy of continual price adjustments to counter inflation. At the other end of the scale 7 companies deliberately held prices constant for periods exceeding 12 months. Another 13 firms claimed that current inflation was self-correcting and could be ignored. Prices would simply be adjusted when the market so dictated. This usually meant also that prices would be held beyond one year. There were 20 firms that made inflation adjustments annually, and 4 made six monthly changes. One firm made three monthly adjustments. Although the effects of even low inflation could erode profits markedly if prices were not adjusted in line, the sample firms presented a not very encouraging picture when 40% of the firms failed to amend prices for inflation within an annual boundary.

It was of interest to record that, as in previous tests, the electrical engineering firms had the better record in this area. Of the 5 companies adjusting prices on a continual basis as a policy, 4 of these were in electrical engineering. When it is recalled that the sample 50 contained twice as many mechanical engineering as electrical engineering firms, this proportion of 4 out of 5 in favour of the latter assumed a definite significance.

Pricing and costs of production

There was little doubt that empirical evidence in general, and that from the South Wessex Survey in particular, strongly supported the view that cost plus percentage pricing was the most common method used for the determination of prices in practice. One major drawback of the method rested on the assumption that firms actually knew what their costs of production were at given levels of output. One could be relatively confident that the closer the firm approached its short run maximum rate of production, the greater became the pressure for rising costs. As the south Wessex firms attempted to squeeze more and more output from their production facilities, a wage premium had to be paid for overtime. If second and third shifts were used the productivity of labour apparently tended to be noticeably lower than on day shift. Constant use of equipment induced more breakdowns, inadequate maintenance and production bottlenecks. Marginal and perhaps obsolete pieces of equipment had to be brought into action to achieve rated capacity. Hiring standards had to be lowered to obtain the labour needed. A loss of some efficiency was therefore almost inevitable at near maximum production rates. Evidence that these results were likely was furnished by the south Wessex firms that seemed prepared to accept these problems in return for a full order book if possible.

No firm in the sample was impressive with its cost attitudes. No firm derived and employed cost curves to assist with pricing despite the majority's use of cost plus percentage pricing. Only 1 firm was able to declare the 'economy drive' as a specific policy. And even if 10 firms could be identified as 'cost conscious' this still left 39 firms without any policy at all for cost curves, cost monitoring or cost saving. Some companies simply assumed that their cost were already at a minimum. Others complained that economy drives were themselves too costly. One respondent did carry out monthly analyses of costs but no decisions ever resulted from these. And a few felt that formal cost policies were only suitable for very large firms. Since many firms in the sample believed that recurring recessions were responsible for returns described as disappointing it might be suggested that cost monitoring could well have been put right by the firms themselves rather than by arbitrary macroeconomic upturns.

It must also be stressed that contribution analysis by the survey firms was conspicuous by its relative absence, and especially among the more successful firms - a point developed in Chapter 9. The importance of this technique could not be over-emphasised yet respondents seemed committed to absorption rather than contribution costing. Since it was not the intention of the South Wessex Survey to concentrate on this subject the point must simply be noted here but not pursued further.

Price and the demand curve

The estimation of revenue or demand curves was a major problem. This was firstly because the level of demand was functionally dependent upon many unquantifiable variables such as personal tastes, and secondly because many of the independent variables which determined the level of demand were highly intercorrelated. In other words, demand depended upon, for example, both the incomes and tastes of consumers whilst at the same time tastes were dependent upon incomes. And, of course, demand for the product could depend upon many other factors such as expected income, other prices, credit availability, legislation, advertising, the consumer's age, inflation, interest rates, and so on. All this implied that the level of demand could only be derived through the solution of a set of equations. But even where past data were available it was not appropriate to employ them for the purpose of demand estimation unless the postulated relationships could reasonably be expected to remain constant over time.

Given the likelihood of errors arising for the reasons outlined above, it was possible in practice to estimate demand curves only subject to a certain degree of error. Further analysis of this problem took us into the area of operations research and hence outside the scope of this work although it might be worth noting that one of the most important tasks of managers concerned with pricing policy under conditions of imperfect knowledge was to assess the significance for the shape of the demand function of small changes in the value of the independent variables on which it depended, known as sensitivity analysis. Very little of this was practised by the respondents in the South Wessex Survey.

It appeared necessary to find out what firms actually did when faced with the problem of demand curves. Evidence from the survey suggested that they fell back on rule of thumb pricing methods. The interviewees were asked to estimate the likely shape of their demand curves for the main product. This turned out to be a fairly imprecise operation. Firms had many different ideas about demand curves, and much confusion. But it was revealed that whilst a significant raising of price would certainly contract demand a marginal increase would not. Similarly, a marked lowering of price would extend demand but a nominal decrease would not. Thus, the demand curve clearly possessed a vertical section at the relevent output level. Firms themselves admitted that price could be raised by a small amount and no sales, in the main, would be lost. Why did firms not take more advantage of this? Clearly, if they did not, then revenue would be lost, profits would be lower than those attainable and returns on net assets would clearly be below optimum.

It should be noted that when price increases were discussed we were referring to economic price increases and not inflationary ones. Obviously, all firms would have to resort to price adjustments in order to counter inflation from time to time, but it appeared that very few firms were prepared to raise price to the point which they themselves knew to be more profitable than any other.

Estimates of possible economic price increases by the firms which would not reduce demand showed that prices could have been raised by 3% to 7% in the short run. Even over the longer term prices could have been increased by 1% to 4% and revenue would have increased.

The finding that the demand cruve possessed a vertical section at the output level in question was considered to be important. If firms knew that by raising price demand would not be reduced why did they not elect to increase profit by this means? As long as firms retained their price, they could not possibly be optimising profit. The goal of survival seemed endemic by this attitude.

The vertical shaped demand curve was probably far more relevant in the real world than the traditionally negative sloping demand curves employed in basic market research. Some support for controlled price increases of the order of those found above might be found in the application of some tests. Assuming that firms wished to raise profits then four basic ways of attempting this were to improve the product mix, increase sales, reduce costs or simply to raise prices. The most neglected method was the product mix approach. Most firms did not know exactly what their costs were. Small firms tended to admit this and even the larger units with more data available might have found much of it misleading. If firms could switch resources into the more profitable lines then this would obviously enhance profit optimality. However, since this policy was unlikely to be applied, at least in the short run, we were left with the three other possibilities.

Increasing sales was a method of raising profits although the firms found it difficult to implement. Apart from the problems of actually finding new customers, there was the difficulty of marshalling resources, and not least, possible overtrading. There was also the problem of liquidity which could mean higher charges for borrowed money. Nevertheless, if the opportunity existed increased sales volume could produce a welcome increase in profits. But it certainly involved much more management and effort than simply raising prices.

Cost reduction tended to have a more favourable effect on profits but, again, it was much more difficult to reduce costs than to raise prices. The action which invloved the least effort produced the best profit results and that was a modest price rise.

The rather specialised nature of one-off producers was examined. Not all the firms were engaged in this type of production since it tended to be quite varied, sometimes complex, and the price was negotiated rather than determined by any other means. In the main, the one-off specialists were able to take even more advantage of the vertical demand curve. The major factor to emerge, however, was that the firms fixed a price after negotiation below the price that the market would actually pay and once again placed themselves in the pursuit of survival as a goal rather than any other.

The point was often put that small firms did not necessarily aim to maximise profits and that financial rewards were often secondary to the satisfaction and independence which was to be obtained from running one's own business. Whilst that might be persuasive it certainly could not, and should not, be used as an excuse for the deficiencies outlined above.

Pricing flexibility

One test of pricing efficiency might be the response of price to some important short term development. For example, did the firms change their prices to take advantage of short run profitable markets? It seemed important to examine short run pricing behaviour as opposed to pricing

that had been determined largely by longer term, and more
traditional, practises. In an attempt to assess the
flexibility of short run pricing decision making the firms
were asked to give examples, if any, where pricing had been
undertaken outside the normal patterns of longer term
pricing policies.

The findings showed responses to be in four major
categories: short run markets via price flexibility could be
pursued but were not (16%); short run markets via price
flexibility were not pursued since other flexibilities were
preferred (62%); short run markets via price flexibility
were not pursued but might do so under crisis (4%); and
short run markets via price flexibility were pursued (18%).

Of the 9 firms pursuing short run markets via price
flexibility, 5 were electrical engineers and 4 were
mechanical engineers. Since there were twice as many
mechanical as electrical engineering firms in the sample
this represented, once again, a significant result in favour
of the electrical engineering population.

Pricing and investment

The debate involving firms' demand for and the supply of
finance for investment purposes as a result of varying the
firm's mark-up policy could be found, for example, in
Harcourt and Kenyon (1976), although it must be noted that
this study confined itself primarily to larger firms.

The focus of the Harcourt and Kenyon work was the link, if
any, between investment and pricing. One element of the
investment decision, its financial aspect, was singled out
as the prime determinant of the mark-up. However, in
principle three main decisions with regard to investment
expenditure might be distinguished: firstly, the amount of
extra capacity to be laid down each period; secondly, the
sort of investment to be undertaken; and thirdly, the method
and cost of finance. The main aim of Harcourt and Kenyon's
investigation was to incorporate all three aspects of the
investment decision into a theory of the determination of
the mark-up. It was presented in three parts. In Section I
the writers stated the problem they were examining in
general terms and listed their assumptions. Section II
contained an analysis of the pricing and investment decision
for a firm where there was only one possible 'best-practice'
technique of production available at any moment of time.
Section III considered the problems involved when the firm
did have a choice between different techniques. The
relationship between pricing decisions and investment
expenditure plans provided a theory of the determination of

the size of the mark-up in cost based theories of pricing. It was assumed that over a range of prices in the short term, prices and quantities were independent. When all aspects of the investment decision were considered including the amount of extra capacity to be laid down each period, the choice of techniques and the method and cost of finance, it was established by the use of a simple model that for the most part, a unique solution could be found for the size of the margin above normal prime costs and the level of planned investment expenditure, given the firm's expectations about the future level of demand. A situation under which multiple solutions might be arrived at was also examined briefly.

Although the work is interesting the impact of price mark-up and investment decision relationships was somewhat reduced in the first instance by the nature of the assumptions. For example, it was assumed that there was one product only, the means of producing output in the short run were taken as fixed, the firm's primary goal was to maximise the growth in the value of its sales subject to a minimum profit constraint, the firm retained the bulk of its profits and the greater part of investment was funded from internal sources.

Since the majority of the south Wessex small firms employed rigid cost plus percentage pricing, and many did fund investment internally, to what extent had the thrust of the Harcourt and Kenyon theory any implications for the smaller firm?

On the one hand the pricing and investment theory established a relationship between pricing and investment, albeit in the larger firm, whilst on the other, the South Wessex Survey effectively rejected this. Only 2 firms acknowledged any possible correlation of pricing and investment and, as far as could be examined, employed this linkage in their decision making.

The relevance of the pricing-investment hypothesis to small firms seemed open to doubt. The South Wessex Survey also revealed that only a small minority scheduled output in response to market forces implying reasonable degrees of flexibility. Any relationship to the mark-up was coincidental. Secondly, most small firms' investment was in the horizontal category and they merely invested when the need arose. The choice between alternative ways of producing the same product was rarely in evidence. It appeared that any link with mark-ups was very weak. And thirdly, small firms had a built in resistance to excessive borrowing even if potentially profitable. Some firms actually practised a non-borrowing policy. As for the cost of finance, small firms' investment appraisals were generally inconsistent with goals of optimisation. Again, any connection with mark-ups was difficult to find. Indeed, the mark-up tended to be fixed arbitrarily. The rate of return on net assets was similarly determined. The mathematical relationship between the two was very largely ignored by the typical small engineering firm.

In short, whilst the pricing-investment relationship might be regarded as important, it would seem to have little application to the smaller firm.

Pricing improvement

The South Wessex Survey had so far demonstrated that when the pricing decisions had occurred in the sample firms it had not really been undertaken with the skill, vision and flexibility required to bring about optimum returns. The respondents were asked to suggest what the firms themselves might have done to make pricing more effective in the raising of profits.

Only 6 firms (12%) had considered the problem but had taken no action to implement the requirements. An even more remarkable feature was the 45 firms (90%) that believed that no action could be taken to improve pricing appreciably since the firm's activities were constrained by such factors as trade cycles, recessions, rivalry in the market and government policy. However, this feeling seemed to decline with increasing size of firm. But the issue of major concern was that no firm in the entire sample had considered how pricing might be improved and had actually implemented the recommendations. It was hardly surprising to find firms preoccupied with survival when such attitudes prevailed.

Of the 5 firms (10%) that had considered how pricing might have been improved 4 were in electrical and 1 was in mechanical engineering. In remembering that twice as many mechanical as electrical engineering companies comprised the sample the latter had tended to overshadow the former in terms of pricing behaviour generally and the position appeared to have been confirmed once again. A sub-sample of just 5 firms, however, could not be regarded as significant. The apparent electrical engineering superiority was a point which could be noted, but no more than that.

Could the lack of initiative regarding pricing improvement be explained? To what extent had the economic climate prevented pricing analysis for improvement? Had the firms ever employed cponsultants to assist with pricing? And what could or should the government do to make pricing decisions easier for the small firm? Atention was then turned towards these areas of influence.

Pricing and the economic climate

During adverse market conditions firms were bound to claim that pricing was affected by future uncertainty. Did the firms take the opposite view when industrial trends were favourable?

Whilst difficult business periods could not simply be ignored it was equally clear that other, and perhaps more basic, factors were relevant. When the total population was taken into account 38 firms (76%) believed that the recession was responsible for their pricing problems to some extent, 4 firms (8%) felt that they had been made to consider their pricing more rigorously, and 9 firms (18%) dismissed the economic climate as a pricing determinant. These 9 companies had taken avoiding action when the recession had set in and had been able to promote sales by means other than pricing. Although it could have been reasonably argued that some of the problems other than the economic climate were also outside the control of the firm, many of the difficulties quoted did seem to be self-imposed, e.g. lack of product development, minimal advertising, no market research and poor delivery performances. The impression was that pricing by many of the firms would have been sub-optimum irrespective of the economic climate. On the other hand, it might be equally be debated that favourable industrial conditions could have encouraged marginal improvements in pricing behaviour but perhaps not beyond that. Moreover, it had to be borne in mind that the findings represented main responses only. Thus, the 76% quoted above could have been under-stated in the sense that the majority of the firms had been unhappy about the economic climate but had not give this factor top priority in their list of pricing hindrances.

Of the 4 firms that claimed the recession had made them consider more effective pricing and had reacted positively, 3 were in electrical engineering. Despite the size of the sub-sample it did reinforce earlier findings that the mechanical engineering firms were seemingly more survival minded that the electrical engineering units. The former's pricing behaviour under recessionary economic conditions suggested that they were more likely to assume that external factors simply dictated conditions rather than to assume that externalities could could be overcome by determined management action.

It was worth noting that the 38 firms (76%) that quoted the economic climate as the main pricing problem were spread fairly evenly between the two employee groups 0-24 and 25-100 staff. The firms had particular views about the consequences of worsening economic trends and they were, of course, supported to a lesser extent by other firms that felt that although their difficulties could have been attributed to more specific factors, the economic situation could not be dismissed.

Collectively, the South Wessex Survey firms believed that local industry was in some respects subject to certain factors beyond the control of individual managements. These factors included fluctuations in world trade supply, prices of raw materials, government policies both in the U.K. and abroad, government legislation, concern about the new business rate with effect from 1990 and inflation around the 6% to 8% mark. These were combining, apparently, to raise a serious lack of confidence within manufacturing industry.

As a result of all this many south Wessex sample firms were working below capacity. This inevitably was giving rise to greater concern for jobs. Every settlement that resulted in wage and salary earners receiving more than the retail price index change caused further anxiety. Additionally, because everything that the firms paid for - labour, materials, fuel, transport, electricity, rates, postal and telephone charges - was increasingly costly, managements were finding it difficult to maintain an adequate level of working capital.

Clearly, it would have been a mistake to underestimate the economic climate's effect on pricing decision making, but at the same time that was by no means the only influence, and in any event the relationship between economic conditions and firms' marketing and investment activity was tenuous.

Must small firms be severely constrained by recessionary conditions? Were there not occasions when the firm itself could circumvent adversity? Why was it that some firms seemed immune to alleged recessions? Once again, it did seem to be the case that most small firms' pricing and related problems could have been solved more by resolute management rather than by arbitrary economic upturns.

Management consultancy

As already mentioned the adoption of rigid pricing methods by the South Wessex Survey firms was not likely to bring about optimum profits. Some 82% of the polulation principally employed the cost plus percentage method of pricing. Only a small minority had looked at ways in which pricing might have been improved. Others believed that little, if anything, could be done to change pricing methods owing to the 'recession' and 'external factors' generally. No firm in the sample had actually implemented pricing improvements in the recent past. Few of the respondents were aware of the required harmony between the target and the mark-up.

Despite the fact that interviewees tended to blame inflation for various problems they were nevertheless largely tolerant of inflation, some only adjusted prices one or even two years in arrear. Contribution analysis was minimal.

If firms had found it so difficult to raise pricing standards, could the problems have been solved by consultancy? The firms were asked if outside expertise had ever been employed to assist with pricing decisions.

Although 18% of the firms claimed that they would be prepared to employ consultants when the occasion demanded, 82% had never used consultants for pricing purposes. And no firm had recruited consultants to assist with pricing difficulties.

Pricing and government

The South Wessex Survey firms were asked to state the most important area of intervention policy that the government might implement and which could make pricing decisions easier for small businesses. A divided attitude could be discerned in that on the one hand firms clearly valued their independence from government control yet, on the other, they expected some assistance from the authorities. The problem was that the firms could not identify what this assistance should be.

Attitudes to government aid revealed that only 10% of the firms felt that government assistance had been helpful. Some 18% had used government schemes over the years but could not link the benefits with the easing of pricing decisions. A significant 38% considered government intervention to be of little help generally, and no help at all with pricing. There were 16 firms (32%) that were largely unaware, or had not taken advantage, of the government assistance available.

The findings highlighted the related problem of firms' being unable to specify what governments could do to ease the burden of pricing. Only 7 firms (14%) had fairly clear proposals to make and these tended to be specific to the firm in question but upon which general policy might be based. Some of these included government consistent policies, more promimnent advisory services, restriction of certain foreign imports, further reductions of governmental bureaucratic demands, more co-ordination with the banks with rescue schemes, more direct contracts with small firms and greater publicity of the assistance actually available including pricing guidelines. Firms considered that these points could, if implemented, impact upon pricing in a favourable light.

Referring to the issue of mechanical and electrical engineering firms, out of the 16 companies that were largely unaware, or had not taken advantage, of government schemes, 13 (81%) were in the former industrial group. Given the composition of the sample one might reasonably have expected that this to be only 67%. The electrical engineering firms, stimulated by their market conditions, were seemingly more active in the pursuit of government assistance. However, it must be emphasised that no firm in the entire sample had considered the area of pricing and government assistance sufficiently to make a rigorous and detailed case for implementation. All the evidence collected suggested that there was no real reason why small firms should not be aware of government incentives that might enable such firms to move away from their survival philosophies.

Summary

The literature on pricing behaviour was inconsistent. In the South Wessex Survey the vast majority of the firms set price by the cost plus percentage method of pricing, an approach unlikely to optimise profits. One-off pricing appeared to be far more flexible. Few of the sample firms were aware of the required harmony between target and mark-up. They were also surprisingly tolerant of inflation, not all firms adjusting prices even one year in arrear. No firm was impressive with its costing attitudes, approaches, systems or general monitoring. Contribution analysis was minimal. A vertical shaped demand curve at the relevant output level emerged from the underpricing approaches of the respondents. Only a minority pursued short run markets by price flexibility. No link was discernible between pricing and investment, No firm in the entire sample had considered how pricing might have been improved and had actually implemented the recommendations. About three quarters of the firms felt that the recession was responsible for their pricing problems. Even though the companies expected government aid, they could not identify the pricing assistance they claimed they required. The survival mentality prevailed throughout, although the electrical engineering firms tended to display the more impressive approach to pricing than their mechanical engineering counterparts.

References

Earley, J. S. (1956). 'Marginal Policies of Excellently Managed Companies', *American Economic Review.*

Gabor, A. (1977). *Pricing: The Director's Handbook*, G. Bull (Editor), McGraw Hill (UK).

Hague, D. C. (1959). 'Economic Theory and Business Behaviour', *Review of Economic Studies*, Vol. xvi, p 144.

Hall, R. L. and Hitch, C. J. (1939). 'Price Theory and Business Behaviour', *Oxford Economic Papers*, Vol. 2.

Harcourt, G. C. and Kenyon, P. (1976). 'Pricing and the Investment Decision', *Kyklos*, Basel, Vol.29, Part 3, pp 449-477.

Haynes, W. W. (1962). *Pricing Decisions in Small Business*, Lexington, University of Kentucky Press.

Silbertson, A. W. (1970). 'Surveys of Applied Economics: Price Behaviour of Firms', *Economic Journal*, pp 542-546.

Simon, H. A. (1959) (1962). 'New Developments in the Theory of the Firm', and 'Theories of Decision Making in Economics and Behavioural Science', *American Economic Review*, June 1959 and May 1962.

Sizer, J. (1971). 'Note on the Determination of Selling Prices'. *Journal of Industrial Economics*, p 88.

Skinner, R. C. (1970). 'The Determination of Selling Prices', *Journal of Industrial Economics*, pp 201-217.

Sowter, A. P., Gabor, A. and Granger, C. W. J. (1971). 'The Effect of Price on Choice: A Theoretical and Empirical Investigation', *Applied Economics*, (3), pp 167-181.

Sowter, A. P. (1973). 'Pricing Models', *Bulletin of the Institute of Mathematics and its Applications*, Vol. 9, Part II, pp 345-347.

Stone, M. (1980). 'Pricing', *Marketing and Economics*, Ch. 10, Macmillan, pp 118-131.

Sweezy, P. M. (1939). 'Demand Under Conditions of Oligopoly', *Journal of Political Economy*, Vol. 47.

Udell, J. G. (1966). 'How Important is Pricing in Competitive Strategy?' *Journal of Marketing*, Vol. 30.

7 Output

Introduction

When examining the goals of firms, sales revenue
maximisation was perhaps one of the most prominent
alternatives to the basically theoretical profit
maximisation. It was, however, surprising that whilst sales
value maximisation has been accepted, sales volume
maximisation has not. Output maximisation implied that
firms chose that level of output where the demand and cost
curves met, i.e. where average cost equated with average
revenue. Just how far output maximisation had been
developed as a strategy for financial optimisation in real
world small firms remained something of an unknown factor.
If firms actively manoeuvred output, and output levels, then
it might be possible to demonstrate that as a result of such
occasional manipulation firms would be pursuing, to at least
some extent, optimisation goals.

Given the above, what were the south Wessex firms' main and
subsidiary products? Why had the companies concentrated on
these products? What degrees of production run were

possible? Which factors actually determined and influenced
output levels? To what extent had the economic climate
influenced output determination? What were the major output
constraints? Was there a desired output level and was this
normally achieved? What was the average level of excess
capacity under normal and recessionary conditions? To what
extent did the firms regard exporting as a major aspect of
output policy? If output had been raised to full capacity,
what would have been the effect on costs, prices and
profits? Did output levels tend to be constant as a policy?
To what degree could firms change output levels to move into
short run profitable markets? What percentage of total
output was accounted for by the customer that took the
largest share? What were the companies' overall investment
strategies with particular reference to output
determination? To what extent had this investment-output
strategy been successful? Which major operations research
techniques did the firms employ? What could the firms do to
make output determination more efficient? And what could
the government do to make output decisions easier for small
firms? These, and related, matters would constitute the
essence of the output determination problem.

Products and production runs

The range of products undertaken by the south Wessex firms
was both wide and in-depth. The areas of business included:
general jobbing engineering, mouldings, steelwork
construction, printed circuits, overhead crane equipment,
air-conditioning units, switchgear, fire control equipment,
spray components, radiator repair, electric motors, heating
equipment, aircraft parts, machine covers, precision
machining, crankshafts, computer systems, electrical
instruments, tensile testing equipment, crystals,
communication equipment, agricultural engineering parts,
acoustic equipment, hydraulics, miscellaneous machine tools,
locks, flexible pipes and specialised clamps. Why had the
firms concentrated on these products and what were the
degrees of production run possible?
It was found that an interesting change of attitude seemed
to occur as the small firm grew in size. Larger companies
were more inclined to acknowledge 'response to demand' as
the reason for their product area. The smaller firms were
the ones that emphasised an 'always having been in the
trade' approach. This latter attitude was perhaps
indicative of certain small firms' philosophy of operation
leaning more towards survival than expansion and innovation.
With regard to the degrees of production run three

categories were devised: category 'A' specialists, category 'B' standardisers and category 'C' repeaters. Of the 50 firms in the sample 26% were in category 'A', 50% were category 'B' and 24% were category 'C'. The main point to emerge from the discussions of production runs was that most firms chose to remain within their categories in preference to the possibilities of extending batch ranges. Certain firms refused to accept one-off jobs. Others felt that large batches would be impossible to handle even with long term planning, and with admitted excess capacity.

Very small firms would clearly find it difficult to extend production categories with their limited resources, but the larger growing companies were in a better position to consider this. The fact that few did so could hinge on the survival approach of most small businesses. Extension of production options would be regarded as a risk and not as an opportunity.

Output determinants, influences and constraints

It could be argued that managing directors were likely to be more interested in maximising outputs rather than profits. Managers would, of course, have in mind a constraint level of profit which would be just enough to keep shareholders satisfied and at the same time make it possible to borrow funds to finance future growth. The company's objective was, therefore, to maximise sales revenue subject to profits being at least equal to the constraint level.

As for the testing of this theory little practical application has been apparent. Any data concerning the motivations behind output optimisation would be useful. With this in mind the South Wessex Survey interviewees were asked to consider those factors which might cause output levels to be other than they would normally be. In short, what exactly were the major output determinants, influences and constraints?

Investigation of this issue showed that customer demand, market conditions, length of order books, repeat orders, government contracts and the economic climate were regarded as the fundamental determinants of output levels by all firms.

Output fixing methods varied according to the size of firm and the industry in question, but three broad approaches could be identified: output levels geared specifically to flexibility, output levels fixed on a semi-rigid system and output levels arranged around a constant policy. Although difficult to analyse in detail these three categories appeared to be fairly strong at the time of interview.

However, it must be remembered that several firms simply had to change their approaches to output determination from time to time if only to realign themselves with current market demands.

Further investigation revealed that 24% of the firms were scheduling output in response to market forces implying reasonable degrees of flexibility. Some 48% fixed output on a semi-rigid system, e.g. by allocating quotas which would be retained until events dictated otherwise. But even more striking was the finding that 28% actually employed a constant output approach. This whole question of output rigidity was important and reference to it is made later.

Influences and constraints were also complex in nature. After output levels had been determined it sometimes became necessary to adjust the targets set, e.g. as a result of unpredictable labour shortages. These temporary short run factors were regarded not as determinants by the firms but as subsidiary influences of output levels. Of course, it might happen that an influence could become a constraint if the shortage of labour persisted, and even a determinant if permanent. Typical contraints quoted comprised inadequate plant, heavy overheads, excess capacity, unsatisfactory quality control, low level of investment, excessively competitive tendering, time consuming output monitoring, inadequate delegation, irregular demand, unreliability of sub-contractors and keeping pace with new technology. However, it was strange that the firms having admitted to these deficiencies were reluctant to accept totally that the blame lay with them.

External factors such as rival activity, government policy, foreign imports, bank credit available and the economic recession, were allegedly major influences of output levels along with the availability of skilled labour. Other influences tended to be specific to individual firms in particular circumstances.

Generally four questions had to be answered by the firms regarding the overcoming of output constraints. Could the product actually be made? Was labour, plant, machinery and expertise available? Was finance, preferably the firm's own, on hand? Was the capacity right? These in essence constituted the major constraints on output levels.

Of the 24% of firms practising some degree of output flexibility, 53% were in electrical engineering and 47% mechanical engineering. Recalling that the 50 firm South Wessex sample comprised 67% mechanical and 33% electrical engineering firms, the 53% result quite clearly emphasised the more progressive output determination nature of the electrical engineering companies in the sample, Part of the explanation for this could lie with their being pulled along by the demands of a high technology market. Moreover, when

the 20 firms that cited external factors as adverse
influences of output levels were considered, only 5 of these
were electrical engineering establishments, whereas the
majority 15 were in mechanical engineering.

The point of this 'determinant-influence-constraint'
section was to establish whether firms deliberately
determined and amended output levels in order to optimise
sales revenue. The results indicated that very rarely did
firms raise or lower output in the short run in a conscious
attempt to optimise sales, profits or even costs. It did
appear that output changes in the shorter term were
motivated more by necessity rather than design. To what
extent this approach actually contributed to sub-optimum
returns on capital, or prevented successful returns from
being higher was difficult to appraise. For example, there
was no evidence that firms failed to complete and deliver
contracts, but this was not to imply that problems of
performance did not exist in this area. There was no
evidence either of firms manoeuvring output other than that
considered necessary by force of circumstance, despite the
failure of several firms to operate at near full capacity.
It was the case that output determination policy was not
awarded high priority by the south Wessex sample firms and
could be construed, once again, as a further confirmation of
small firms' survival aspirations.

Output and the economic climate

The south Wessex respondents made it clear that the main
determinant of output was current demand conditions. This
view was expresssed by 82% of the sample. They also
indicated, yet again, that external factors, including 'the
recession', were prominent in the output decision. Some 40%
made this point strongly. Whilst the interviewees were able
to identify specific output catalysts, the 'recession' was
never remote from the discussion.

As in other aspects of business activity, external
conditions clearly affected the decision to promote output
at least to some extent. However, it was obvious that
internal factors within the control of the firms were, in
the main, equally relevant. Nevertheless, from the total
population 74% felt that the recession (or alleged
recession) was the principal cause of their various output
problems.

It would, of course, be fair to emphasise that some
external issues were indeed beyond the firms' control, but
on the other hand, it could be put that several problems
quoted did appear to be self-generated, such as lack of

basic marketing, inadequate plant capacity, absence of advertising and so on. Self-admitted inadequate plant capacity over the years could hardly be described as a recession imposed problem. Output determination by many of the firms would surely have been sub-optimum whatever the economic climate. Perhaps favourable conditions would have stimulated marginal output growth but hardly more than this.

It should be noted that the findings obtained were main responses only. Thus, the 37 firms (74%) that quoted the recession specifically was almost certainly understated in that the majority were concerned about recessionary conditions but did not necessarily give this factor top priority in their hierarchy of output hindrances.

It would be an error, however, to understate the economic climate's impact on output decision making. Conversely, this was certainly not the only factor for many south Wessex firms, and in any event it was suggested in the answers given that the relationship between economic conditions and output levels was tenuous. If the economic climate were assumed to be represented by, for example, the money supply, retail price index, bank base rates, industrial growth, etc., there was a definite lack of harmony between these factors and the output of the firms in question. It seemed that most small firms' output difficulties would have been eased not so much by an improvement in the economic climate but by more far more positive management application to the output determination problem.

Of the 15 firms claiming to have overcome the recession by various means, 8 companies (53%) were in electrical engineering. The remaining 7 mechanical engineering firms (47%) represented a below par result given that 67% of the full sample comprised these firms. It appeared that the electrical engineering units had responded to the recession in a more purposeful manner than their mechanical engineering counterparts. The electrical engineering sector was one in which output promotion and development had to keep pace whereas the the mechanical engineering market did tend to be somewhat more static, especially under adverse conditions. It was probable, in view of the evidence, that the mechanical engineering firms relied too heavily on the uncontrollable external factor as an excuse for sub-optimum output activity.

Output and excess capacity

An optimum size of plant or firm might be defined as that size of unit that has the minimum average costs of production in view of its demand conditions, the supply situation of the factors of production, relevant government involvement, e.g. taxes, and any other issue placing strain on, or giving advantage to, the firm. This suggested that optimum size might not be a given size, but possibly a range of sizes.

As far as the south Wessex firms were concerned two questions seemed important in the assessment of output efficiency. What was the average level of excess capacity? And if output were raised to full capacity, what would happen to costs and prices? Maximum excess capacity had been estimated by the firms and was inevitably presented as an average over time. But care was taken to ensure that the figures quoted were indicative of the extra output the firm could produce without recourse to overtime working, excessive demands upon machinery, management and finance. Similarly, the amount of capacity required to produce subsidiary products, if appropriate, was also an approximation. Finally, the results of the raising of output to full capacity were restricted to the effect upon costs, profits, prices and productive efficiency, although other points were noted such as growth, job security, reduction of fixed costs, and so on.

Practically every firm in the sample had experienced some degree of excess capacity over the recent past and occasionally these unused resources had amounted to 50% and over. No firm could claim zero excess capacity on a continuous basis.

An examination of the responses revealed that 64% of the firms recorded excess capacities of 10% and over, whilst only 36% could claim that unused resources were normally below 10%. A rather high 12% admitted to excess capacities of 50% or over. The average level of excess capacity for the whole sample was 16.38%. The average for the electrical engineering firms was 13.75% and 17.7% for the mechanical engineering companies. A point worthy of note was that the very small firms in the sample were the ones that suffered less from excess capacity than their larger contemporaries. Interestingly, although not part of the study there did not appear to be any correlation between the level of excess capacity and the achievement of the target rate of return on net assets. For example, some firms in the survey with virtually no excess capacity reported that they sometimes failed their targets, whilst others were successful, and vice versa.

The decision to accept subsidiary work, and one-off jobs too, was not always based on profit. Several reasons were given why this type of work was undertaken: to maintain the work flow, to supplement routine work when excess capacity was high, to explore the possibilities of routine production contracts from one-off prototypes, to gain potential customers, to aquire experience, expertise, etc., in that line of production and to increase profit. The point at issue was whether spare capacity was available or not. It has been observed that in the majority of cases, it was. Moreover, it was also discovered from most of the interviewees that if capacity had been raised to the 100% level then unit costs and possibly prices could have been held and even reduced involving the firm in little or no financial hardship. Thus, spare capacity was not only available, it would also have been profitable to eliminate. But the firms seemed reluctant to take advantage of certain profitable opportunities preferring to maintain the survival profile so readily observable in the various forms of decision making undertaken by the south Wessex sample firms.

Further investigation showed that 16 mechanical engineering firms (32%) had excess capacities of below 10% whilst 12% had unused capacities of 50% and over. It was of interest to compare these figures with those obtained for the electrical engineering companies. Some 46% (23 firms) had excess capacities of less than 10%, and only 10% of the firms had unutilised capacities of 50% and over. Once again the latter appeared to outperform the former.

Output rigidity

One test of the small firm's efficiency might be its ability to secure a continuous flow of work. Delivery, price and quality were the key influencing factors. In the south Wessex sample there was an emphasis on price rather than on delivery and although the latter was regarded as important simple progress charts, for example, were not in evidence.

Effective output operation also needed a minimum level of work in progress to ensure continuous production. This was generally well understood by the firms but what was much less well appreciated was that the occasional overfilling of the system was potentially just as damaging as underfilling it.

Balanced scheduling of output was required for effective operation but perfect synchronisation was, of course, impossible because both the volume and the work content were volatile. In certain firms chronic imbalance seemed to be an accepted part of the total system. The section of the workplace that was constantly under capacity was readily identified by the firms as the creator of the bottleneck, but this excess capacity was far more likely to survive correction. Recognition of the cost of meeting peak loads at different points in the system was vital, but the majority of the firms did not give this very much priority.

Successful output fixing required rather more thought than simply allocating fixed quotas of work to departments, sections and individuals. A certain flexibility was needed to avoid the pitfalls above. Unfortunately, the firms lacked this degree of planning, in the main. Indeed, the typical small firm appeared to simply wait for an order to arrive and then allocate output quotas subject to certain plant constraints. The outcome of this was basically a confirmation of output rigidity.

Some decisions by the sample firms affected the nature of demand and therefore the timing and sizes of batches required from the production lines. It was apparent that many so-called fluctuations in demand were created by the various links in the distribution system, each in turn exaggerating an initial minor variation. A rigorous look at forecasting and stockholding might well have shown that greater and more stable output could have been obtained if modifications had taken place. On the one hand, whilst the case for evening out unnecessary demand fluctuations, and actually promoting a reasonable degree of output stability might be acknowledged, on the other hand this was not to argue the case for the 14 firms (28%) that employed output rigidity as a policy. It was also not to argue the case for output rigidity beyond the shorter term.

Did output levels tend to be constant as a policy even in the firms claiming otherwise? To what extent could the firm change its output level to move into short run profitable markets? What percentage of total output was accounted for by the customer that took the largest share? What magnitude of price change would motivate a change in supply? These questions were put to the south Wessex firms. Taking the last question first, it was found that significant changes in price would affect levels of output, but marginal changes would not. Thus, the supply curve had a vertical section indicating rigidity at the output level in question. This vertical section coincided with the vertical section of the demand curve already identified in the discussion on pricing.

The vertical nature of both the supply and demand curves at the relevant output level made for output rigidity at least over the short run. The chances of output levels being raised or lowered in response to changes in price depended more on the extent of the change rather than on the specific desire to optimise returns by means of output manipulation.

Where outputs were not constant, a majority of the firms claimed resulted from 'uncontrollable external market conditions' rather from the internal policies and decisions of the firm. Only 3 firms (6%) seemed, as far as could be discerned, to be actually pursuing a positive flexible output policy, and could clearly demonstrate this. Of the

12 firms (24%) mentioned earlier claiming this output flexibility distinction, 9 of them were not quite as impressive as the 3 companies singled out above. In some cases the 9 firms were engaged in output flexibility by accident rather than planning. Flexibility had to be resorted to, for example, in order to complete contracts on time

Many of the firms suffered from excess capacity yet had few plans to eliminate this, e.g. by market flexibility, product development, advertising, and so on. Up to 40% of the firms clearly relied far too heavily on the repeat orders of large customers. The importance of these contracts was emphasised by the sample firms in terms of the familiar theme of survival. Survival did not have to be negative. It could have been applied to the survival of the firm in an expanded, improved or more efficient sense, e.g. to avoid take-over. Regretfully, too many small firms regarded survival simply as remaining in business at a minimum level of operation.

Output and investment

Most firms would want to establish some control over the markets in which they operated. The very small firms obviously would have rather less influence in this respect. Growth via strategic investment appeared to be a way forward. Greater penetration of markets would offer the firm that extra market power. Moreover, if small firms were concerned about survival (and many of the south Wessex firms were) then purposeful investment could also be a means of achieving some degree of security. And even if these two reasons were to be rejected by some smaller firms investment could always be undertaken if only to produce enhanced personal rewards. The development of a profitable business by an owner was in itself an example of personal achievement. Clearly, an output-investment policy would widen the range of opportunities available to the small south Wessex firm. Quite often the worth of a firm was measured not so much by current performance but by investment growth potential.

Consequently, the sample firms were asked what the investment strategy was with particular reference to output determination, and to what extent this strategy had been successful.

Only 5 firms (10%) could be identified as practising direct, planned, visionary output-investment strategies, and it was the larger units that predominated here. Twenty one companies (42%) appeared to have no direct, indirect or planned output-investment strategies at all.

It was evident that the respondents did not, in essence, see any direct links between output and investment. It was equally clear that the firms had not necessarily rejected the idea of such joint strategy, but had simply not considered the possibility. There tended to be more emphasis on indirect links, if any. If indirect linking was accepted as a 'strategy', to what extent had this produced successful results?

Although 10 firms (20%) could claim varying degrees of success as measured in their terms, no firm in the entire sample could state that output-investment monitoring had revealed highly successful results.

Out of the 5 firms with direct planned output-investment strategies, 4 were in electrical engineering (which must be regarded as a significant result despite the small sub-sample) indicating a more progressive attitude by these companies towards the output-investment relationship. In general terms the electrical engineers appeared to be ahead of the mechanical engineering firms as far as the output-investment linkage was concerned.

Output techniques

The south Wessex firms were asked to specify the most important output 'operations research' techniques employed. Even allowing for the fact that the nature of the industry and the type of production undertaken could influence this it was notable that 33 firms (66%) could indentify no techniques considered to be indispensible for the company's efficient operation.

A minority of firms only, i.e. 6 (12%), were employing output techniques of an acceptable standing on a continuous basis, i.e. output scheduling, critical path analysis, stock control and quality control. However, these techniques were being employed more on a casual rather than rigorous basis. The larger firms were prominent in the awareness of these techniques. It was the smaller firms that argued the inapplicability of output operations research techniques. The 14 firms (28%) either using output techniques continuously or on an ad hoc basis were all in the 25-100 employee group.

Certain firms felt that the installation of a micro-computer constituted the employment of output techniques. Of the sample 50 firms, 35 (70%) were using computers for various purposes including, for example, output monitoring. Just 12% had purchased computer aided design packages. The impression was that this 70% was a rising trend despite some reservations by the firms about computers.

There were basically three opinions about microcomputers. The micro installed simply failed to do the work that was expected from it. The micro installed did the work expected but usually in one half day and the problem was what to do with it for the rest of the week. No micro had been purchased because there was no real need and the management had heard of problems experienced by other firms.

Simply by way of comparison, as long ago as 1970 the Engineering Training Board employed the Bristol Polytechnic Small Business Centre to survey a sample of engineering companies employing up to 200 people in four regions in England. The report selected 14 management techniques and a 79 company sample. Most respondents were able to declare the usage of one or more techniques but since these included job description, cost centres, productivity bargaining, etc., as well as quality control, production scheduling, critical path analysis, stock control, etc., a more impressive response than the South Wessex Survey of 28% using output techniques alone was inevitable. Indeed, the report concluded that there was a usuage of 50% on average by the firms in the sample consisting of generally larger firms than the south Wessex population. It has already been noted that it was the larger firms in the south Wessex sample that were engaged in output techniques. There might well be some measure of agreement between the two studies. This agreement may, or may not, be significant. Further research is obviously required into this specific area. It was true that some south Wessex firms considered that output techniques could not always be applied, but even so that could not excuse the absence of, for example, basic demand estimating and quality control. The overall picture would tend to confirm the impression of non-optimal behaviour by firms far more concerned with survival than output growth. Some of these firms had actually identified areas where output techniques could be introduced, but had made no progress regarding implementation.

There were 14 firms (28%) that were either using output techniques on an ad hoc basis, or continuously. All these firms were in the higher 25-100 employee group, but more significantly 8 were in the electrical engineering industry whereas, given the composition of the sample, one would have expected only 4 or 5 to have been part of this sub-sample.

It seemed that the small firm's slowness to introduce output techniques was unjustified. Some firms had adopted output techniques successfully and had demonstrated their applicability. Similarly, some firms' reluctance to employ microcomputers was shown to be unnecessary by other firms that had installed computers with satisfactory results.

Output improvement and consultancy

The South Wessex Survey revealed output determination problems within the small engineering firm. The respondents in some instances had actually confirmed these shortcomings. Could the firms themselves suggest what might be done to make output decisions efficient and effective? Had the interviewees ever employed outside expertise to assist with output difficulties?

Investigation revealed that if output improvement had been implemented it was by the 25-100 employee group firms. Some support for this finding could be found in the fact that of the 19 companies (38%) that had not given any consideration to output determination improvement, 13 were in the 0-24 employee group. The larger firms seemed to be rather more conscious of output determination improvement than the smaller ones.

Moreover, the employment of consultants was a rarity. Only 7 firms (14%) had used outside expertise for specific output determination purposes. Another 7 firms (14%) stated that although consultants had not been used they might be employed if the need arose. Therefore, 36 firms (72%) had never used consultants, because they considered that their services were simply unnecessary. They had also no intention of changing this attitude. Given that many of the south Wessex firms were preoccupied with survival the findings had to be regarded as unfortunate if not surprising.

There were 5 firms (10%) that believed output determination to be adequate because, for example, output was already at full capacity. This was an interesting instance of firms believing that change was unnecessary if a system appeared to be working at that moment in time. The real test came when the system was under pressure. The consultant would argue that improvement was always possible, and change should occur before the pressure occurred rather than in response to it.

There were, however, 5 firms in the sample that had implemented output determination improvements, and another 11 that had plans for improvement. Out of these 16 companies, no fewer than 8 (50%) were in electrical engineering, representing a significant increase on the 33% that might be expected from the sample. Also, of the 7 firms (14%) that had used consultants for output determination 5 were, again, electrical engineering units. It was almost impossible to suppress the impression that the electrical engineering companies were responding positively to market trends in various ways, not least in output determination, whether on own initiative or by consultancy. As for the firms not kindly disposed towards consultants

they would have been well advised to take advantage of the
relevant services available, and not pre-conclude that
consultants were too expensive, disruptive, inventors of
problems and representative of external interference.

Output and the role of government

The 50 respondents of the South Wessex Survey were invited
to comment on the possible role of government regarding
output determination decisions in small firms. Several
problems arose. On the one hand small firms welcomed
assistance from government, but on the other, generally
preferred less intervention. Secondly, even if assistance
were established, interviewees could not easily state
precisely what that help should be.
A highly significant 38% of the sample (19 firms) believed
that government aid was generally too little and too late.
Another 34% (17 firms) were basically unaware of the aid,
schemes and advice available. The well over 200 measures
introduced between 1980 and 1991 to help small businesses
were, for the most part, unknown. However, some 10% (5
firms) had received indirect help from government, e.g. in
the form of Ministry of Defence contracts placed with large
firms which had then been sub-contracted to certain south
Wessex firms. Only 18% (9 firms) could claim that
government intervention had been directly relevant to output
determination.
The problem of firms being unable to indicate what
governments might do to ease output determination
difficulties was apparent. Only 6 firms (12%) had specific
ideas in this area, and these tended to be individual in
nature. However, national policy could possibly be based
upon them. Some of these included government consistent
policies, more prominent advisory services, restriction of
certain foreign imports, further reduction of governmental
bureaucracy, more co-ordination with the banks with 'rescue'
schemes and much greater publicity of the assistance schemes
available. But it had to be noted that, in the main, firms
were doubtful about the real effectiveness of government
intervention in the small firm sector. The reaction of
small firms to government incentives was more likely to be
responsive if the assistance impacted directly on output
rather than initiatives that promised indirect, delayed or
unidentified results. If the authorities were to bring in
measures designed to ease the output determination decisions
of small firms, then the recommendations would have to be
well publicised, understandable and have immediate impact.
The south Wessex firms were largely unable to offer any

applicable suggestions as to what form these recommendations might have taken.

Out of the 16 companies that were unaware of government schemes, 13 were in mechanical engineering. Knowing the composition of the sample to be twice as many electrical engineering firms as mechanical, the reasonable assumption to be drawn was that this might have been expected to be only 11, i.e. 67% of 16. The electrical engineering firms, stimulated no doubt by the nature of their market opportunities, were seemingly more active in the pursuit of government assistance. However, it must be repeated that no firm in the entire sample had considered the area of output determination and the role of government sufficiently to make a detailed case for implementation.

All the evidence available suggested that there was no real reason why small firms should not be familiar with government aid which might well enable such firms to shake off their survival mentalities.

Summary

Real world output optimisation literature remained undeveloped. The south Wessex sample firms appeared to be reluctant to extend production beyond known products, being regarded more as a risk than an opportunity. Very rarely did firms deliberately amend output levels in order to optimise sales revenue. Output changes in the shorter term were motivated more by necessity than design. Some external issues, whilst clearly beyond the firms' control on occasions, tended to be used as an excuse for lack of management ideas and action. Output determination by many of the firms would probably have been sub-optimum whatever the economic climate. Excess capacity varied between 0% and well over 50%. If capacity had been raised to the 100% level by management initiative, profitability would have ensued. Firms, however, simply failed to eliminate their spare capacities. Output rigidity generally prevailed and only a very small minority were pursuing a positive flexible output policy. Market research, demand estimation, advertising, product development and exporting were all accorded surprisingly low priority, especially by the smaller firm. It was evident that the respondents did not, in the main, see any direct links between output and investment, and only 5 firms out of the 50 sample could be identified as practising direct, planned and visionary output-investment strategies. Few firms were employing output techniques of an acceptable standing on a continuous basis. Some 70%, a slowly rising trend, had installed

microcomputers. The employment of consultants remained a
rarity. Reservations about consultancy were probably very
much over-stated in the light of the evidence available. A
highly significant percentage believed that government aid
was generally too little and too late. About one third of
the firms was basically unaware of the government assistance
available. Interestingly, firms were largely unable to
suggest what the form and nature government aid should
actually take. The South Wessex Survey revealed endemic
problems of output determination but the electrical
engineering firms emerged with some credit in the various
'tests' undertaken. Undoubtedly pulled along by the nature
of a volatile and demanding market, they demonstrated an
encouraging response to these challenges. The mechanical
engineering companies were less so inclined. There was
little correlation between the employee groups 0-24 and 25-
100 and productive activity. But in terms of philosophy of
operation a clear message was apparent - that of survival.

References

British Institute of Management, (1972). 'The Needs of the
Manager in the Small Company', *Bristol Branch Discussion
Paper No. 1*, June, p A7.

8 Marketing

Introduction

It has been observed that, in the main, the South Wessex Survey small firms under review operated sub-optimally in their investment decisions, price setting and output determination. The survival goal prevailed and this adversely affected decision making. Did this problem apply across the board or was it confined? Were there other areas of management activity that were similarly affected? The investigation consequently turned to an examination of marketing attitudes. For example, what were the firms' marketing policies? Did the firms employ qualified marketing staff? How well established was training? Was employment creation related to marketing? To what extent was market forecasting in evidence? Was any market research employed? Did the firms engage in significant product development? What were the attitudes towards advertising? Was any priority accorded to packaging and distribution? How much exporting occurred? Did firms concentrate on developing their service to customers? Had the economic climate influenced marketing decisions? Had government initiatives made marketing decisions easier for the firms? Were any management techniques employed, e.g. quality control? Could the respondents themselves suggest what might be done to make their marketing more effective? To what extent had consultants been employed to assist with marketing problems? What was the extent of information technology regarding marketing? And did purchasing and supply relationships exist? These comprised the main areas of inquiry.

Marketing policies

The interviewees were asked to state the firms' marketing policies. Only 10% quoted sales expansion but some 38% had no real marketing policies at all. Others mentioned reliance upon repeat orders, striving for product quality, maintaining local reputation and attracting larger customers. Only 12% felt that exporting was a major aspect of their marketing priorities although one firm had received the Queen's Award for exporting. Conceptions of marketing success included only 14% claiming significant sales expansion, and only 24% declaring the generation of adequate profits. When the main marketing problems of the 1990's were explored, 14% complained about the lack of skilled labour, 12% were worried about increased competition, but 24% experienced the problems of lack of orders or irregular work flow. Overall it was mainly a question of ad hoc marketing decision making in response to current demand. Policies, if they existed, were more reactive than proactive. There were several reasons for this state of affairs, e.g. traditional methods employed by owners, lack of financial resources and reliance on existing local markets. But another factor concerned the quality of the marketing staff employed.

Marketing and training

Some 40% of the firms employed no qualified marketing staff and the vast majority of these had no plans to change the situation. A 'marketing officer' or 'marketing director' was employed in 16% of cases, whilst the 'managing director acting as marketing officer' comprised 26%. It must be emphasised that practically all of these had no formal marketing background. Only 6% of the sample had an official marketing department. Many of the respondents felt that there was no need for formal marketing. In examining the marketing education and training of other staff more closely, 78% had none and most of the remainder could only claim a marketing knowledge not beyond that necessary for normal production and routine selling. Marketing appeared to be the yet another neglected area, among other aspects of business, in terms of formal training.

The firm's labour force was regarded by the management as the most important asset it employed, and it was acknowledged that shortages of suitably qualified staff across the board, and especially in marketing, could affect the financial performance of the company. The sample firms seemed to suffer unduly from such shortages of skilled labour because of their relative lack of purchasing power in the labour market. The firms' attempts to overcome this problem fell far short of formal training. Very few employees were engaged in training at the time of investigation. Day release for a minority of staff was the most popular outlet. This required personnel to attend the local college to gain qualifications. Surprisingly, this was dominated by technical and technologist grades rather than managerial. Short course attendance on a commercial or college based scheme, however, was a significant method for managerial and clerical people.

For many years small firms have complained about the lack of skilled labour. Large companies too have experienced similar problems. In the latter case though training programmes were more likely to be in evidence than in the former. Indeed, even at the onset of the 1990's the consultant is sometimes hard pressed to uncover any form of meaningful training in the smaller company. It is pointed out that to take on labour is in itself risky. To train that labour only to see it competed away by the larger firm can be both expensive and frustrating for the small entrepreneur. In reality the position tends to be that little or no marketing, or other, training is availble at all. Some basic 'on the job' or 'hands on' training might have been offered in order that certain machines could be operated but this would not compare with a well planned inductive and systematic training programme. The very small firm argues that it cannot afford training, once again regarding it as a cost rather than an investment. Whilst there might be some sympathy with this view it could never be a substitute for the training now urgently required for the next ten years and beyond.

The respondents were asked if they had a structured induction and on-going training programme in operation. Only 8% could claim they had and could demonstrate its existence. Some 76% of the south Wessex sample had basic 'hands on' training which was, in the main, simply implemented as and when required. By their own admissions

16% of the firms had no training at all. In some instances there were no regular trainers. Occasionally, staff were asked to induct or demonstrate without notice. Few of these staff had training backgrounds or qualifications in the subject areas such as marketing. Hardly any firms had specific policies of staff training by in-house seminars, conferences, short courses, etc. And no firm had ever employed consultants to advise on training and training needs.

When asked if the company had in-house seminars to discuss training, or even other matters, the results were equally disappointing. Only 18% held regular in-house training seminars, 44% held them only when necessary and another 38% never met at all for training discussions.

Did the firms have a specific policy of gaining up to date knowledge of marketing techniques, new technology, etc., by regular staff attendances at conferences and courses? Only 12% of the sample had such a policy in place, 40% claimed that they would be willing to send staff to conferences and courses as necessary, but for nearly half the firms a programme of regular attendance was not given any priority at all.

Of the 62% (18% + 44%) of the firms that had pursued training and knowledge of new developments, what were the main topics selected? From a rather rambling list the following were the most popular. Computing (22%), Health and Safety (18%), Industrial Relations (12%) and Finance (14%) were prominent. Management of Change (8%), Just in Time (6%) and notably Marketing (6%) were not at all well represented.

These results tend to reinforce the whole problem of training. Too few firms took advantage of the training opportunities offered. Interestingly, no firm in the entire sample had asked staff to attend courses on '1992'.

Had the firms employed consultants to assist with their training? No firm had employed consultants for marketing training or, indeed, any kind of training thoughout the period (1980' to early 1990's) under review. Small firms react best to the one to one face to face relationship. On the one hand consultants must be prepared to spend time engaging in this practice, whilst on the other the small firms themselves must learn to appreciate the advantages of expert external assistance.

The findings also highlighted the very small firm's vulnerability. In every test in this survey the firm with between 0-24 employees was inferior, in the main, to its larger counterpart. Almost certainly these are the firms that require training programmes the most.

One problem encountered during the investigation was that some employees regarded attendance at conferences and courses as 'time off' or as 'a break from work'. Certain staff believed that where they had been on a course a yearly follow up would have been appropriate but this rarely occurred. Others felt that induction, if any, usually covered far too little ground for far too short a time. Generally speaking, small firm management tended not to have an appreciation of staff training needs. Consequently, training was basically ad hoc across the board. One further point must be stressed. Staff themselves were not always over enthusiastic about training despite its 'holiday' appeal. Perhaps a relevant and rigorous training policy initiated by the south Wessex firms would have catalysed a more positive response from staff. Often the reporting back from courses was minimal or non-existent. Staff claimed not to be aware of the tasks undertaken by other departments, and particularly with reference to marketing. There was certainly very little training in the sample regarding jobs carried out by colleagues. At least one might have expected some interchange of staff between departments from time to time, but there was a negligible degree of such transfer. The survey confirmed that labour was the firm's most valuable asset. Effective training could only enhance that asset. The smaller firm's persistent neglect of this area of management could prove to be one of the major problems of the 1990's, although it must be emphasised that some of these staff attitudes were initially encountered by the writer as long ago as 1977. Clearly, little has changed.

Employment creation

The encouragement of small firms has been a priority of government assistance for some time. In part this has been seen as a means of easing the problem of unemployment. The policy has been based upon evidence of real job creation in smaller firms, especially those that were growing rapidly.

However, certain studies have questioned this job creation. Two problems have been highlighted. There has generally been insufficient knowledge of whether small firms create jobs or not. There has also been a lack of data regarding the types of jobs small firms create. In essence there were six questions to have answered. Did small firms create jobs in aggregate? Were the number of jobs created fewer or greater in aggregate than expected? Was there a single reason for the contribution to employment by the small firms in question? Did the jobs created by the firms possess varying degrees of quality? Was it the fast growing firms that created most of the jobs? And did the smaller firms display a low employment creation rate?

Of the 50 firms interviewed there was no one size of firm responsible for the majority of job creation. Indeed, there was relatively little job generation overall. One reason for this was the inability of the firms to recruit the required skilled labour, including marketing staff. Another reason was the policy of some firms actually to reduce labour in favour of the introduction of allegedly high technology. There was no evidence, however, of the laying off of staff as a result of this. A third reason was that the late 1980's and early 1990's represented a relatively high employment base rate compared with the early 1980's.

During the investigatory period of the 1980's and early 1990's only 1.76 new jobs on average per firm per year had been created - 88 in total per year. But over half these new jobs were offset by staff resignations. Moreover, some 50% of these jobs were estimated to be relocated ones. And some 59 jobs had been generated by just six firms. Another sixteen firms created 35 jobs, whilst twenty five firms created no jobs at all, and three firms contributed job losses of 4. Given these results it seemed most unlikely that the firms would appoint marketing staff as net new jobs. The chances of each firm having its own marketing officer was equally remote.

The picture could not be described as optimistic. There were fewer jobs created in aggregate than reasonably expected, in that just six firms generated 60% of the jobs. Five of these six companies were in electrical high technology engineering, although of different sizes. All six claimed that expansion of the market and their response to it had contributed significantly to their recruitment of labour. But no firm had employed staff for marketing purposes.

Moreover, no firm in the entire sample claimed that jobs had been created in order to prepare for likely future developments. All firms invested in labour simply when the need arose and not in anticipation of future growth in key areas, e.g. marketing.

It must be noted that the jobs created by the firms varied in quality from managerial to shop floor unskilled. Fourteen appointments were part-time, of which twelve were semi-skilled to skilled.

The six companies that had created 60% of the jobs were growth firms but not excessively so. Indeed, some of the firms that created no jobs had similar growth rates, that is in terms of output, profits, sales, exports, investment, etc. In these cases the installation of new equipment was a notable feature of their operation but this action was not balanced in any way in terms of marketing appointments.

Market research

Market forecasting was not a requirement actively pursued by the firms in question. About 50% of the sample were able to state that market forecasting was not popular because it had learned from experience that it was 'impossible', especially under the recessionary conditions of the 1980's, and particularly the 1990's. The other half had simply not given any attention to the problem. It had just not been viewed as an aid to marketing.

Only 6%, just 3 firms, of the survey population were engaged in active market research and another 24% on an occasional basis involving the managing director's 'expertise' rather than trained marketing staff. Despite the fact that many firms in the sample were local, a discouraging 70% undertook no market research of any kind. What the customer really wanted had also not been tackled with any degree of rigour. Most firms argued that the market was known. Customers approached the company with orders and the firm responded. It was claimed that there was no need to research customer wants. Consequently the size of potential markets remained unknown.

Product development

Out of the sample 50, only eight firms (16%) were engaged in continuous and identifiable whole and new product development. Another 22 (44%) claimed to develop new components or to refine existing products on an occasional basis but this was less obvious and difficult to verify.

What was clearly observable was that 20 firms (40%) had not been engaged in product development of any kind over the years. And even the 60% involved, or claiming to be involved, in product development to some extent (with the electrical engineering firms tending to predominate here), were nevertheless operating at a sub-optimum level given their approaches to product development generally.

Much of the product development was more reactive than innovative. For example, just over 60% of the respondents felt that there was a shortage of funds (internal and external) for new product development in the U.K. But in terms of investment, as stated earlier, external finance tended to be avoided by the firms.

This somewhat introverted investment approach almost inevitably undermined progressive product development. Yet respondents complained of the lack of funds for new products. There was a certain neutrality concerning the question that the small firm sector was characterised by many entrepreneurs with limited experience for product development. On the one hand it was claimed that product development expertise existed, but on the other hand the lack of actual product development could not easily be explained. The vast majority felt that consultants were unlikely to be helpful for product development purposes, especially at the level of fees charged. This was entirely consistent with the general attitude towards outside advice.

The firms were critical of the government assistance available for the development of new products. However, very few companies (22%) could identify specifically the extent of product development aid and assistance in recent years. In most cases it was clear that the lack of government aid feeling by the respondents had been reached without supporting evidence.

Uncertainty prevailed regarding the difficulty or otherwise in selling new products. Since new product development was inclined to be at a sub-optimum level, this unsureness was not too surprising. Very few firms had entered the new product development field, yet felt that there must be severe difficulties at the selling stage. The majority (66%) agreed that when a recession ended the firm tended to abandon new product development in order to manage the resurgent demand. Many (78%) considered that small firms had little option in this respect. While this might represent a degree of flexibility to take advantage of new opportunities, it also demonstrated adverse flexibility as far as product development was concerned. Managers agreed that where product development occurred, the new product was expected to have a market growth far above their firm's recent sales performance.

This approach was broadly in line with the setting of targets by the firms themselves and then, in the main, failing to reach them. Had more product development been undertaken it was possible that the continual experience gained might have made product development expectations not only more realistic but also more likely to be realised.

Respondents (74%) believed that any proposed new product would obviously fit in well with their present lines of products. This was seen as an advantage and as an indication that the firm could integrate new products successfully. It was also regarded as a means of keeping clear of risk-bearing diversification. The majority (62%) also agreed that, for the proposed new product, their ability to develop this line in the very short term was critical to its acceptability.

Given the firms' preoccupation with survival, it was not easy to accept that they would be sufficiently adaptive in the very short run to succeed with product development.

Where new products had been developed over the years (16%

of the sample only) the majority, from a technological point of view, regarded the product strategy that the new products represented as 'comparative advantage', a key to entering a new product class and as a move towards a more highly finished product.

On the other hand, the majority of the 42% claiming to be involved in component improvement or existing product fine-tuning felt that, from a technological point of view, a new product idea would be 'revolutionary'. Normally this group was involved, at best, with updating or enhancing current parts. There was general agreement in the product development firms that with regard to product production factors a new product idea could be seen as economically feasible.

The component improvement group tended to view a brand new product idea as economically less viable. But 82% of the whole sample concurred that once developed, a new product would be expected to serve a market or customer need not previously satisfied.

While firm conclusions were difficult to reach from this qualitative data it appeared that despite only 16% being engaged in rigorous product development, most respondents realised the true value of product development and the benefits for the firm.

There was a basic awareness of the importance of feed-back in that for the new product early market research data flow clearly indicated whether the new product was likely to succeed or fail.

There was agreement that in terms of corporate goals the new product represented, or would represent for the component improvement group, a good fit with management preferences, and could be seen as an aggressive in-house new product idea.

Finally, the sample firms saw no relationship between product development and job generation. If the development of products required the recruitment of extra labour, then this would have to occur. But product development policies were not regarded as a means of employment creation. Product development tended to generate jobs for the firm in question, albeit not deliberately. It was likely, however, that these were not new jobs but merely relocated ones.

Product development seemed to be recognised as essential for progress by the firms but some respondents with few opportunities for product development tended to dismiss it. The alternatives of developing service, speeding up delivery dates and improving existing product quality had not been given serious consideration. Interestingly, several firms claimed to possess the facilities and the expertise to develop their own product. Yet the problem remained that this potential had not been, and was unlikely to be, realised.

Advertising

The firms were asked to state their advertising policies. Only 18% were able to reveal policies that were based upon an 'advertising expenditure and expected related returns' approach. Some 24% advertised occasionally as the need arose and held that this was their 'policy'. However, 58% had no real advertising policy at all.

Of the firms pursuing specific advertising policies (18%) the effectiveness of these was especially difficult to assess. Further research in this area was clearly required. A number claimed that responses to their advertisements over time had been disappointing.

Were the firms advertising in the most optimum quarters? Interestingly, 86% of the sample had apparently not analysed rigorously the effectiveness of their own advertising.

A highly significant 40% of the firms did not employ fully qualified marketing or advertising staff. A 'marketing officer' or 'marketing director' was in post in 16% of cases, whilst the 'managing director acting as marketing officer' comprised 26%.

The vast majority of these staff had no formal academic marketing or advertising backgrounds. Only 6% of the sample had an official marketing department. Many respondents believed that there was no requirement for formal marketing or advertising

A few companies in the survey, most notably the larger firms, spread their service efforts too thinly by attempting to do too much. There was little evidence of firms concentrating on what they could do well, such as full customer service, specific product specialist, etc., and advertising these.

Other firms (62%) whose service might have been improved tended to feel that their business record had been satisfactory since: 'Customers have not complained'. None of these firms had attempted to advertise this perceived successful service. Only 20% were prepared to look at service, further improve it and ultimately advertise it.

Practically every firm in the sample had experienced some degree of excess capacity throughout the 1980's and early 1990's. From time time these unused resources had amounted to 50% and even over in a few firms. No firm could claim zero excess capacity over the longer term.

Firms themselves admitted that if production had been raised to the 100% level then unit costs and possibly prices could have been held, involving the firm in no financial hardship. Spare capacity could have been profitable to eliminate by a host of policies, not least advertising. But the firms remained reluctant to pursue such a policy.

The response that full capacity working would have been readily undertaken if contracts had been available was not necessarily a valid point for a competitive firm to make. For example, to what extent did the firms actively seek out new business possibilities and move into and out of reasonably accessible markets? The finding was that very few interviewees could confirm that this was done as a specific policy of the firm, although many considered that market seeking, for example by advertising, could be a profitable venture.

It was quite strongly held that small firms did not actually need to advertise. It seemed that the across-the-board problems of the typical small firm could almost certainly have been eased by the application of the basic advertising skill lacking, by implication, in the findings.

To be effective for the firms in question, advertising had to be specifically targeted to generate active responses. It had to stand out, identify the name of the product, the name of the business and provide a promise of a benefit to the customer, whilst also being consistent with the image of the business and other forms of promotion.

To achieve objectives advertising had to be of high quality and the preparation and the production of art work and display material should have been professionally produced. It would usually be worthwhile to commission an advertising agency to handle the work and target the relevant markets.

There could be a choice from national, regional and local newspapers. Yellow Pages, trade magazines, consumer magazines, local radio, cinema, television, mail shots and poster and transport advertising. Furthermore, sales promotions, incentives, competitions, free offers, discounts and demonstrations would be useful supportive methods.

Advice from the various consultancy bodies, for example the Small Firms' Service and the Department of Trade and Industry, would normally be available.

Sponsorship was another relevant form of sales promotion involving sports, arts and other companies. The use of editorial coverage and articles in trade magazines covering new products could be employed in some cases. Of all these advertising posibilities raised with the sample firms, the majority demonstrated interest in the discussion of these, but a minimal interest in their possible implementation.

As far as sales constraints were concerned, as perceived by the firms, inadequate plant capacity predominated along with the lack of skilled labour. The recessionary economic climate, as indicated previously, was also regarded as a constraint beyond the control of the firm. At no point was advertising singled out as a possible weapon against these contraints by either the mechanical or electrical engineering firms.

Exporting

A quite different set of contraints apparently prevented exporting. There was, as usual, recognition by the firms that exporting could be a crucial element in enhancing business performance, but there was significantly less acceptance of the need to actually integrate exporting into their marketing policies.

Of the firms in the sample only 4% were exporting over 20% of their total output, another 8% exported between 5% and 20% of output, and a further 20% exported occasionally but less than 5% of output But notably, 68% had not sold abroad at all. The majority of these companies, incidentally, fell into the 0-24 employee category rather than the 25-100. It appeared to be the case that the larger firms were more export minded although from a low base. Additionally, there was no distinction between the mechanical and electrical engineering companies in this respect.

Why should the export records of the south Wessex firms be so poor? Most of the firms were content with the home market despite alleged and real recessions throughout the 1980's and early 1990's. This attitude was entrenched in their basic approach to business and was unlikely to change easily.

Secondly, many of the companies claimed to serve local markets predominantly and had established reputations for quality products, service and reliability over the years. Exporting would draw heavily on resources currently needed to fulfil local demand.

Thirdly, most firms believed exporting to be fraught with pitfalls including legal requirements, currency complications, language difficulties, etc. The sheer effort required for successful exporting was not considered to be worthwhile for very small firms.

Fourthly, some pointed out that they exported 'indirectly' in that their products, or part products, were ultimately exported by the customer. This proved to be difficult to verify.

Two firms revealed that they had exported in the past but the results had been most unsatisfactory not least from unfortunate dealings with agents in the overseas countries.

Were the non-exporting firms justified in their attitudes against selling abroad? Was exporting feasible for the small firm? Of the 16 firms that were exporting at all, 6 claimed the activity to be 'highly profitable'. Eight companies assessed the outcome as 'satisfactory'. And just 2 firms had been 'disappointed', but would certainly continue to export. The indication was that despite the obvious limitations of a sub-sample of 16 there was no reason why exporting should not be successful given, of course, that the procedures were followed, specialist advice taken and the mechanics of exporting were carried out effectively. Too many of the sample firms had rejected exporting too readily and especially since some of the companies had excess capacities which could have been utilised for exporting. Unfortunately, the firms simply did not feel the need to seek out possible overseas markets.

This finding that small firms made little effort to find lucrative markets was not too surprising. Small companies are not renouned for market research, forecasting, advertising, product development. etc., even within the home market. Clearly, if they were to research markets abroad they would require some assistance.

Had the firms ever approached export consultants to advise with exporting? Of the 50 firms interviewed only 3 had engaged consultants for export purposes. Indeed, hardly any of the companies had employed consultants for any purpose, as indicated previously. And even where advice had been sought on occasions this had been at an elementary level, e.g. advice regarding government grants, interviews with the bank manager, discussions with accountants, etc. There were no actual consultancy contracts and where recommendations had been made by bank managers, accountants, etc., hardly any of them had been implemented, mainly on the grounds of expense. In fact very nearly all of the firms felt that consultants for exporting purposes, or otherwise, were expensive, disruptive, interfering and just inappropriate for the small firm. It did appear that the small firm in question had blatantly rejected consultancy when the advice available could have been crucial for a successful exporting launch.

For successful exporting to result the firm must essentially follow a critical path through the map of available opportunities. For example, firms may have never exported before because they did not know how to proceed. Yet there are numerous advice centres to assist with guidelines and documentation. Firstly, the firm must attempt to identify markets abroad that would be suitable for the firm to enter. Market intelligence is required. There may be social, political and cultural problems to explore as well as economic. The fact remains that the export division of the Department of Trade and Industry is a crucial starting point. There is also the British Overseas Trade Board, the British Market Research Bureau Ltd., the British Export Houses Association, not to mention the embassies of foreign countries, the City Business Library in London, the Financial Times special market surveys and statistics produced by Her Majesty's Stationery Office and trade associations. Secondly, the financial aspects of exporting must be understood. Credit insurance should be taken on all exports. Such insurance is available from the commercial sector as well as from the Export Credit Guarantee Department of the Department of Trade and Industry. The Export Credit Guarantee Department as well as the banks offer assistance regarding export procedures. There is no shortage of help. Had any of the sample firms availed themselves of this assistance?

Just 16 firms were involved in exporting and only 6 of these exported to any significant extent. It was surprising to learn that not all had used the facilities available. Only 7 had approached the authorities for expert advice despite the fact that some of the counselling was free of charge. Once more the insular survival attitude of the typical small firm was apparent. In most instances there was not even an interest in the possibilities of exporting. With 1992 looming the position seemed inexplicable.

Marketing and information technology

Although the four principal areas of management covered by the south Wessex survey, i.e. investment, pricing, output and marketing, all lent themselves to computerisation, it was the latter that was given priority of examination. Had the firms adapted information technology to their marketing activities?

Of the 50 firms under review 70% had a computer installed, the most popular type being the standard microcomputer used by 44% of the sample. Only 16% of the companies employed a mini/main frame computer. The home computer was also not well represented, only 12% had one. The finding that 30% had no computer at all in 1991 was perhaps both surprising and disappointing even though many of the firms in question were quite small in the 0-24 employee bracket. Nearly all the firms with computers of some kind had fundamental attachments such as V.D.U's and disk drives. Only 20% had colour printers. Other 'attachments' such as laser printers, modems, mouse, etc., were employed by some 40% of the firms. The most popular reason for installing a computer by 48% of the users was to save time in the marketing function. Strangely, the least popular reason for installation was to be more accurate. Only 16% claimed this. Some responses to this question did tend to be rather individual: 'to keep up to date with modern marketing developments and requirements', 'to follow the leads of other companies', etc., were typical examples.

Of the 30% of firms that did not currently own a computer 62% claimed that they did not intend to purchase one within the foreseeable future. For the remaining companies the most popular type of computer they thought they would purchase was either a mini/main frame or a microcomputer. The firms without computers were asked to give reasons for non-installation. Some 86% thought that a computer system to cover their marketing activities would be simply too costly. Other reasons were that the firm was just too small and would not benefit from the introduction of a computer, turnover was too low, there was no appropriate marketing software to fit requirements and it was too late to learn about computers.

Over one third of the firms (40%) that currently owned a computer introduced it with particular reference to marketing, although not exclusively, between 1 and 5 years ago. Moreover, 26% of the sample installed computers between 6 and 10 years ago, 20% between 11 and 15 years and just 4% over 15 years ago, whilst 10% had purchased their computers within the past year, i.e. 1990 to 1991.

Some 68% of the computer firms had recently upgraded their hardware. The remaining 32% had not, although many of these had only recently purchased their computers and thought it unnecessary to upgrade them so soon. There were examples, however, of a minority of firms that purchased computers some years ago, i.e. between 5 and 10 years, and had not upgraded and had no intention of doing so within the next 2 years. Some firms were not sure if they would upgrade or not. Of the firms intending to, or might, upgrade, 16% would upgrade the whole system, 50% would upgrade in part, and 34% were unsure how the upgrading would proceed.

Of the 35 firms (70%) owning a computer 5 firms would not reveal the amount spent on the purchase. Thus 30 firms provided the following information:

```
16% spent under     £1,000
32% spent between  £1,000  and £5,000
22% spent between  £5,000  and £10,000
14% spent between  £10,000 and £50,000
 8% spent between  £50,000 and £100,000
 8% spent between  £100,000 and £500,000
```

Interestingly, if the cost of computerisation above is compared with the size of the firm using the number of employees as the citerion, there is not a directly proportional link. There is, however, a cluster of points which suggests some correlation between the size of the business and the amount spent. In three cases though, larger companies in the sample purchased relatively cheap computers.

With regard to the type of the firms' first software package, of the 35 firms owning a computer, 15 of these firms chose to purchase a word processing package before any other, 7 chose a sales ledger first, 6 bought a computer aided design package and 7 opted for a collection of miscellaneous software packages which they considered would be helpful with their marketing and other activities. The most common first package was word processing, a vital package that from the firms' point of view enabled letters to customers, reports, etc., to be prepared more easily. In one firm the computer was used solely for label printing since the business - a very small firm - had no other use for the computer. Indeed, the impression was that computerisation was somewhat under optimised by most of the firms.

Some 23% of this sub-sample of 35 firms took seller reputation into account when choosing software packages. Only 20% considered low cost as an essential ingredient of choice. Compatibility was quoted by 17%. Another 17% believed that 'organisational fit' was important. Only two firms (6%) felt that value for money was the main reason. And 6 companies (17%) admitted to no particular reason at all for software purchase.

Thirteen firms (37%) claimed not to have experienced any major problems with their software packages. But 17% felt that training had been a difficulty; 11% found the packages 'inappropriate' for their requirements; 11% had problems with power; and another 11% had suffered from 'bugs in the system'. Other obstacles comprised: keyboard and/or printer problems (6%); difficulty in finding programs (6%); and lack of manuals (6%). As in most instances in this study these findings represented dominant responses. Some firms, of course, had experienced several of the problems mentioned above but to varying degrees.

Only 43% of the firms had software application packages tailor made for their purposes. Of these 15 firms, 7 stated that they had bought packages to suit individual needs; 4 firms based their purchases on personal recommendations; 2 firms obtained the tailor made package on a 'one program was required and one was purchased' basis; and 2 firms had no particular reason for the acquisition.

Over half of the firms owning computers, i.e. 19 out of the 35, admitted to some disruption during the implementation of the technology into the workplace.

Apparently, no disruption was suffered by 12 firms (34%), and 4 firms (11%) could not indicate whether disruption had been experienced or not. Some of the problems included: disruption of work from necessary reorganisation of established working routines, compliance of personnel, lengthy learning periods resulting in losses of productive time and the setting up of the system.

The introduction of computerisation for marketing or other purposes had required inevitable training, but in only 26 firms (74%) of the 35 firms in question. It must be noted that it was difficult to appreciate just how the remaining 9 firms had coped seemingly without training. Some of the training offered consisted of 'reading from the manuals', but most of the instruction came from teaching by computer specialists from outside the firm, training by competent fellow workers and knowledge from attendance at occasional courses and formal training sessions. The impression was that the firms preferred, in the main, to have their staffs taught by outside experts, a finding that seemed to contradict the typical small firms' appreciation of consultants generally. The length of training periods varied, but most of the companies preferred short intensive instruction, sometimes covering only one or two days.

By no means all of the firms were aware of the health and safety issues affecting computer users. Fewer than one third knew that the length of continuous time at a computer was an important consideration. Only 17% (6 firms) were aware, for example, of the possible risk to pregnant mothers using a V.D.U. screen. Layout of room, regular eye checks for users, light levels, etc., were other examples that some of the firms had simply not observed.

Whether for use in the marketing context or otherwise, some of the small firms in the sample with computers appeared to have bought equipment they did not really need and ended up with virtually an expensive typewriter. There was little doubt that businesses can be influenced unduly by advertising into accepting that computers could 'solve' their business problems. In reality the computer itself can comprise a problem for the unprepared small firm. Inappropriate advice can occasionally persuade firms to invest needlessly in computerisation. The effective use of computers demands a disciplined commitment, not least to training. Perhaps the smaller firm would benefit from a sound manual marketing system as a first stage? The survey revealed that businesses were often ignorant of how restrictive a computer could be. If there was only one skilled operator in a small staff the difficulties here were self-evident. Moreover, learning to use the computer seemed to be as costly as purchasing the system in the first place.

The output from computers can only match the input. Given this truism, manual systems for firms, and especially small ones, can be the vital underpinning for this data input. There is little doubt that manual systems have improved over recent years, and many systems now allow rapid anlaysis for up to date management information. Almost certainly some of the sample firms had not given these points due consideration.

Purchasing and supply relationships

Why do firms engage in partnership practices? There could be several reasons, e.g. direct or indirect economic interests connected with an increasing awareness of environmental responsibility, the need to develop an image, the belief that partnership could be a positive factor for the business climate generally, a means of expanding the research and development base, to share expertise and, perhaps not least, to pool certain risks in the marketing field.

However, in the south Wessex sample only 4 firms (8%) were able to demonstrate an attempt, if no more than that, at informal partnership with larger purchasers and suppliers. This was largely based on the fact that the small company in question was somewhat over committed to a major purchaser in terms of the percentage of output produced. It was almost a necessary imposition. The remaining 92% (46 firms) appeared to have given the purchasing and supply relationship little serious thought believing that high interest rates for small firms despite occasional reductions in base rate (of the early 1990's), the new uniform business rate, lack of skilled labour, competition, difficulty of securing orders, etc., were far more important considerations.

For example, inbound logistics (receiving, storing, inventory control and warehousing) and outbound logistics (collection, storage and distribution) had not been communicated in any way to purchasers or suppliers by the sample firms. They, in turn, had never requested purchasers or suppliers to advise them of their logistic procedures. Indeed, in some cases there appeared to be a conflict of procedures that negotiation could have eased.

Moreover, few of the sample firms had queried the service offered by purchasers and suppliers and they had not, in most instances, questioned the service provided to them. Thirteen of the firms (26%) worked to BS5750 and felt that this in itself was an aspect of guaranteed quality.

Suppliers were not researched to any noticeable extent by the sample companies. Most of the suppliers were known to the firms and they believed there was no pressing need to investigate. Yet 23 firms (46%) claimed to have been let down to varying degrees by suppliers in the recent past and agreed that researching might have avoided these problems. Despite this, the firms had not been ruthless enough with unreliable suppliers. If a contractor quoted a delivery date the firms simply accepted this - they did not research it. Five firms admitted, however, that certain large major purchasers did research them.

In essence there was little partnership communication between the firms and their purchasers and suppliers. Where power clearly resided in a major purchaser the sample firm could see little prospect of developing partnership under such conditions.

The placing of contracts with purchasers tended to revolve around price. Once price had been established (Stage I) then delivery, fine tuning of design, quality, etc. (Stage II) followed. Partnership attitudes were far more apparent at Stage II than at Stage I. The sample firms suggested that partnership barriers clearly existed and pricing was an example of this. Apparently, one could negotiate in a partnership frame of mind more freely on design, quality, etc., but much less on price.

The respondents reacted to change 'as required'. Little or no preparation had been undertaken for 1992, possible 'Just in Time' with partners or general partnership ideas across the board.

One company in particular had over 1,000 suppliers. Its relatively few purchasers were large and prominent. The firm claimed that it was familiar with these purchasers by their reputations, and was content with this. On the other hand, their 1,000 suppliers were largely unknown in partnership terms. The firm was dependent on its large purchasers. It was less dependent on its 1,000 suppliers. Therefore, the partnership relationship could afford to be weak. The possibility that some of the 1,000 suppliers could have been dependent on the sample company was not thought to be a major issue by the firm. Obviously, there are limits to backward integration. This could be both expensive and a long term commitment. The firm was not specifically looking for new, or even better, suppliers. It preferred to rely on the existing ones. The search for the new supplier tended to be occasional. Partnership was felt to be inappropriate by the firm. The cutting down of the number of suppliers and the targeting in on quality and reliability of supply involving partnership had not been considered by the firm, or indeed, by most of the other firms in the south Wessex sample.

There was little evidence of the firms offering subsidies to assist their suppliers to meet requirements. Contracts once placed were left to the supplier to comply with and deliver. Discounts had been offered to purchasers from time to time but this practice was more in line with necessity rather than partnership.

With regard to purchasers and suppliers' systems, the sample companies had not researched how they might integrate their own systems and procedures in partnership. There was, as expected, an awareness of 'Just in Time' by all the firms. All thought that they should be moving towards this although at different levels and paces. Unfortunately, it was believed that purchasers and suppliers would simply not co-operate, although this had not been investigated. Long run changes would be needed and the sample firms were not optimistic about unknown longer trends. Basic forecasting, for example, as earlier pointed out, was considered to be especially difficult. It was also stated by most of the interviewees that small firms had to operate on a day to day basis since long term indicators tended not to exist. The external market and the economic climate determined a host of activities and decisions for individual small firms and the partnership ideal could not readily fit into this pattern. Twenty three firms (46%) felt that partnership would most likely catalyse conflict rather than harmony.

If partnership were established with purchasers and suppliers, co-ordination of, for example, investment, pricing, output, marketing, advertising, training, product development, etc., would be expected to develop albeit to varying extents. But the sample firms demonstrated a major problem here. The attitudes to decision making were conditioned principally by the necessity criterion. This confined the firms to operate at an insular level which rendered the prospects of partnership remote.

Investment policies were mainly non-visionary, inflexible, based on ploughback profits rather than external finance, repairs and maintenance, etc. None of the firms claimed to be interested in the investment plans of purchasers or suppliers.

Even pricing policy was only relevant at the contract stage. It was not the policy of the firms to involve themselves in the pricing behaviour of their purchasers or suppliers.

On the marketing side, as already noted, there was little evidence of market research, market forecasting, market departments or even qualified marketing staff. It was apparent that these fundamental deficiencies would need to be tackled before any suggestion of partnership could be pursued.

Very little advertising was undertaken. Trade journals, Yellow Pages, etc., seemed to be the extent of the advertising function. Some firms preferred the 'knock on door' method. No firm in the entire sample had researched which advertising was actually best for them. Not surprisingly, purchasers and suppliers' advertising was of minor consideration to the firms.

Training too was at a disappointing level. 'Hands on' or 'on the job' training was in evidence but systemised, meaningful, programmed training was not. Hardly any reporting back from conferences or courses occurred. Inevitably, the firms were not concerned with training, if any, in the purchaser or supplier firms.

A small minority of firms was engaged in product development although even this had a necessary safety element involved. The remaining firms had either occasionally developed products, or part products, when the need arose, or there was no product development at all. Most of the firms had the expertise to develop products but failed to do so as a specific policy, even though the excess capacity persisted. To take an interest in purchasers and suppliers' product development was not high on the list of priorities.

The interviewees regarded expenditure on market research, advertising, training, computing, etc., as a cost rather than an investment. Consequently, there was a general tendency to adopt an inward directed economising approach to decision making. Partnership would require an outward looking co-operative approach with the emphasis on investment benefits available rather than the pre-occupation with expense. Given all this, the sample firms were clearly not at this stage. They were not primed for partnership.

Summary

Marketing decisions were mainly ad hoc in response to current demand. Policies, if they existed, were more reactive than proactive. Some 40% of the firms employed no qualified marketing staff and only 6% had an official marketing department. Some basic 'on the job' or 'hands on' training was in evidence but well planned inductive and systematic training programmes were not. The sample firms regarded training as an expense rather than an investment. No firm claimed that jobs had been created in order to prepare for likely future marketing or other possible developments. Of the jobs actually created over half had been offset by staff resignations, and about 50% of these jobs were, in any event, estimated to be re-located ones. Market research was not a requirement actively pursued. Only 6% were active in on-going market research. In most cases the size of potential markets remained unknown. Only

16% were engaged in continuous and identifiable new product development. Much of the product development was somewhat less than innovative. Product development was recognised as essential for progress but too many firms with seemingly few opportunities for product development tended to dismiss it too readily. In terms of advertising 58% had no real policy despite unacceptable levels of excess capacity. The recessionary economic climate was regarded as a constraint, among others, beyond the control of the firms but at no point was advertising singled out as a possible weapon against these contraints. A quite different set of contraints apparently prevented exporting. Of the firms in the sample only 4% were exporting over 20% of their total output on a regular and sustained basis, with 68% not selling abroad at all, believing exporting to be fraught with pitfalls. Surprisingly, only 14% had approached the advisory bodies such as the Export Division of the Department of Industry and Trade, regarding export procedures. Although beyond the scope of the South Wessex Survey, being worthy of separate research in itself, the sample firms were remarkably unaware of the Single European Act, when the SEA came into force, the aims of the SEA, how the SEA has affected Economic Community decision making and, not least, the effects of the SEA concerning, for example, free movement of goods and services, the protection of the environment, VAT and the of the SEA for small firms. With 1992 looming the position seemed inexplicable. Seventy per cent of the companies had a computer installed but its underuse was clearly apparent. A computer purchased for no more than word processing was virtually a waste. Just over one third introduced computerisation with particular reference to marketing. Information technology training was adequate at best. Most of the training was cursory and in some cases non-existent. The smaller firms would probably have benfited more from a sound manual system rather than expensive and under utilised computerisation. In theory there were sound reasons why firms would engage in partnership practices with purchasers and suppliers. However, in the south Wessex survey only 8% were able to demonstrate an attempt, if no more than that, at informal partnership with their purchasers and suppliers. It was found that partnership would require an outward looking co-operative approach with the emphasis on investment benefits available instead of a pre-occupation with with expense. The sample firms were not at this stage of development. They were not primed for partnership. In demonstrating the deficiencies of the small engineering company it was notable throughout that the very small units and the mechanical engineering firms were generally inferior with few exceptions to their larger and electrical engineering counterparts. Finally, in practically all instances the firms had blatantly rejected consultancy when the advice available, occasionally free of charge, could have been crucial for an enhanced business performance across the board.

9   Performance

Introduction

Could the performances of small business units be forecasted
and measured? An attempt was made to do this with the south
Wessex firms and some usable if fundamental results were
obtained.   However, a marked contrast could be observed with
the characteristics for forecasting corporate performance
concerning, for example, the small hotel sector on the one
hand, and staffing as a management responsibility on the
other.   Whilst there were definite similarities regarding
managerial attitudes, behaviour and approaches to problems
with all three areas of investigation there were certain
barriers against model building with the latter two.

Forecasting corporate performance

During the course of the South Wessex Survey an attempt was
made to determine those qualitative characteristics, if any,
of the small firms under review that might act as predictors

of financial performance (Gillingham, Hankinson and Zinger 1987). The essential premise was that while predictive models based on financial data are available in the literature, the building of a set of organisational and managerial attributes that could could be linked to superior results might provide a prediction of the small firm's future survival. The attributes selected for examination included, for example, utilisation of marketing research, formalisation of the planning process, reward systems and union-management relations.

It was hypothesised that companies identified as being 'successful' might possess 'common attributes' that singled them out irrespective of their obvious differences. The research undertaken here was intended to find out if there existed a consistent relationship between managerial attributes and performance. It seemed likely that reliance solely upon quantitative data for forecasting purposes might be unwise. Firstly, as Gillingham, Hankinson and Zinger (1987) point out, because such information is derived from the firm's financial reports, questions are inevitably raised concerning the comparability of the ratios in so far as substantial latitude exists in terms of the generally accepted accounting principles which govern the preparation of financial statements. Moreover, in accordance with the reality of a dynamic business environment wherein operating conditions are subject to constant change, such usage of financial ratios seemed more suited for analysis after the fact. The example of a south Wessex firm producing low profitability owing to heavy commitment to research and development that would place it in competition with its rivals is a case in point.

In reality, absolute values do not exist for factors such as organisational design, product or market focus, or production effectiveness, but by examining the trends of the South Wessex Survey firms it was hoped that it might be possible to highlight some basic features and policies that were evident in successful companies yet were clearly lacking in others.

The management practices and policies investigated in the South Wessex Survey could be divided into broad categories:

    Research and development
    Planning and control
    Marketing policies
    Financial management
    Personnel
    Operations management
    General management policies

In addition, certain basic organisational traits were also

of some interst and many of these would be classified as
uncontrollable factors including such considerations as
growth rates of major markets, the average age of the
management team, government regulation and the degree of
utilisation of committees in the decision making process.
    While the survey addressed a number of specific issues in
each of the above categories those factors which were
expected *a priori* to be observed most consistently in
successful corporations and to be clearly linked with
relatively superior financial performance included:

    Well defined budgeting system
    Ability to determine readily, contribution margin
        attributable to specific products/market areas
    Well developed market research programme
    Adequately funded advertising programme
    Formal day to day cash management procedures
    Formal procedures for evaluating capital investment
        proposals
    Ready access to outside funding
    Emphasis on management training and development
    Utilisation of profit sharing schemes
    Modern production facilities
    Utilisation of management science techniques

It was expected that these factors in particular would
represent situations that generated success.
    The 50 respondent companies were divided into two groups
based on their self-assessment of their rate of financial
return over the past 5 years (1986-1991). Those with an
average return of less than 15% on capital per annum were
declared to be 'unsuccessful'. Those with 15% or more on
average were classified as 'successful'.

Figure 9.1   The most significant attributes of more
              successful and less successful companies

	Percentage of this group having this attribute	
	Less successful companies	More successful companies
	(31)	(19)
Rating lowly the importance of the objective of rational- isation	74	89

	Percentage of this group having this attribute	
	Less successful companies	More successful companies
	(31)	(19)
Rating less highly the importance of the objective of consolidating gains made	52	84
Rating more highly the importance of the objective of long-term growth	35	79
Less likely to have formal plans used in the organisation	16	58
Less likely to feel constrained by a lack of financial resources	61	89
Less likely to use committees to take actual decisions	26	68
More likely to use experience in various functions as a training method	48	79
More likely to have seven or more people reporting directly to the key person	16	42
More likely to have capital projects reviewed within a capital budgeting framework	45	84
Less likely to be able to identify the costs incurred and the financial contributions made by each department and/or area/division	32	63
More likely to use management science techniques	6	47
More likely to assess their firm's productivity as above that of their competitors	48	84
More likely to asses the age of their facilities as younger than their competitors	45	79
More likely to assess the quality of their physical plant as above that of their competitors	58	84

	Percentage of this group having this attribute	
	Less successful companies	More successful companies
	(31)	(19)
More likely to be offering fewer products or services than their competitors	6	42
More likely to make purchasing decisions at a higher level	29	74
More likely to value highly the views of sales and technical representatives in determining consumer needs and market opportunities	39	74
More likely to organise their marketing on the basis of geographic area	39	63
Less likely to use last year's budget as a basis for this year's	48	84
More likely to place some importance on export markets	39	68

Sources: South Wessex Survey 1991
            Gillingham, Hankinson and Zinger (1987)

The two groups were compared using the wide range of attributes as shown in Figure 9.1 above.   This figure provides a characterisation of the more and less successful companies on twenty variables.

It appeared that the more successful firms placed less importance on consolidation and more on long-term growth. Surprisingly, they were less likely to have formal plans and were less likely to be able to identify contribution levels from each departmental area.   They were less likely to use committees to make decisions.   The overall impression was that the more successful companies were more likely to be market orientated, offer a small range of products, to have a leaner staff and a more intensive appraisal of capital projects.   They were also more likely to have newer, more productive and higher quality plant and equipment.

The research provided some evidence that successful firms were distinguishable from less successful companies because of their managerial attitudes and attributes. These differences, once fully understood, might well prove useful to managements in improving their own organisational performances. The use of forecasting techniques based upon these factors might also be of interest to those practitioners involved with predicting corporate financial performances. Needless to say that the nature of the data required by this analysis suggested that managerial factors were most likely to be used by the firm's own management team rather than by external analysts who would not necessarily have immediate access to such information.

The results suggested strongly that a small number of managerial factors could possibly predict the financial performances of companies and provided further supportive evidence for the general hypothesis that managerial factors were the primary determinants of a firm's success or failure. In the main, although analyses of the small and larger firms and of the mechanical and electrical engineering companies in the sample could be be meaningfully undertaken here, the attributes indicated that the successful companies were characterised by objectives which focussed on positive features such as exporting, market research, etc., rather than upon negative factors such as conserving the present situation or rationalising operations.

Small hotels

Despite the endemic problems of small firms exposed in the South Wessex Survey it was at least possible to collect data that enabled the forecasting of corporate performance findings, above, to be produced. However, by no means all small businesses lend themselves to such an investigation. Some small businesses have virtually no organisational structure or managerial and/or financial discipline. The very small hotel is a case in point and provides an interesting contrast to the small engineering firm. Indeed, in many ways the behaviour and attitudes of small hotels reinforce the discoveries of the South Wessex Survey. But the small hotel sector simply defies the collection of data for the building of a 'forecasting corporate performance' model.

The Hampshire coastal region of the U.K. is a tourist area of historical interest, scenic countryside and attractive coastline. The emergence of the hotel industry over the years was the natural response to the inevitable tourism expansion, and the small hotel sector in particular was predominant in this development.

Quite separate from the South Wessex Survey this section describes a study of 30 of these small hotels, with up to 25 beds only, in south coast Hampshire. All units in the sample were interviewed in the same open unstructured personal method. The investigation covering the period 1986 to 1991 revealed some serious problems of investment and related sub-optimality across the board.

Most of the hotels (73%) had persisted with their own methods of operation over the years and had not considered any critical change of approach regarding, for example, staff training, computer installation, enhanced service, external borrowing for investment purposes, advertising, etc. The flexibility that might be expected from the small hotel, and the small engineering firm incidentally, was absent in most instances. Current demand was the fundamental determiant of operations rather than any initiative by management to attract business, especially in the off-peak season.

It transpired that the principal goal of 23% of the hotels was reasonable profit. Subsidiary policies were of an individual nature such as safety, maintenance of reputation, labour cost savings, etc., but two clear aims repeated themselves, as in the case of the small engineering firm, satisfactory profits and survival. These were claimed to be the only possible objectives for very small hotels given recurring recessionary economic conditions. The policies though, did seem to be the result of historical or traditional decision making and once the small hotel had selected a goal this would be retained and only amended when events necessitated. Since the hotels considered survival and satisfactory profits as foundations for success the signs indicated that the owners were simply aiming to remain in business and no more than that. Many of the hotels regarded survival alone as 'success'

Just over 50% of the population had been in the hotel business for under 6 years, and 33% for less than 3 years. Relatively few owners, i.e. 13%, were from the local area. The majority (40%) had moved in from south east England. Hardly any owners (7%) had formal qualifications in the hotel and catering trades. Most (37%) came from the skilled non-manual and skilled manual groups. The majority of the enterprises were very small in scale, 63% having an annual turnover of less than the current VAT registration level (around £24,000 on average) over the 1986-1991 period, and 70% were under £40,000 over the period. Most (53%) employed only a minimum of staff from outside the owner's family. Only 27% of establishments engaged more than two people on any basis. And 20% employed no outside staff at all. Some

of the owners actually had outside jobs themselves.
Attitudes of owners towards training were poor. For the
family members hours of work were long, or at least long
hours of work were claimed. Only 23% reported that they
were working fewer than 50 hours per week, The problem of
distinguishing between 'hours of work' and 'hours on duty'
posed a problem in research terms. Prices charged
throughout the sector were low and 73% of the sample were
charging less than £15 (1986) and less than £20 (1990) per
night per person in the high season. Some 27% charged £10
or less on occasions, it was claimed. Local competition was
the major determinant of price rather than the facilities
that the hotels offered. Profitability was clearly sub-
optimum as a result, not unlike the small engineering firm
situation. The majority (67%) had a crude policy for future
development, but this was not well formulated or part of any
wider business planning. General refurbishing was the main
priority for future investment, and survival. Current VAT
(£21,300 to £35,000 during the 1986 to 1991 period) was
major consideration in respect of business plans and 60% did
not consider it worthwhile exceeding the VAT limit. Some
63% had not registered for VAT. Marketing policies by 90%
were virtually nil. Most establishments used the local
guide book for advertising. Many relied upon passing trade
in areas of high hotel and guest house concentration.
Finally, the hotels' aims were 'family orientated' rather
than 'business' and as such the enterprises under review
were clearly operating, in the main, well below optimum.
    As with the small engineering firm in the South Wessex
Survey, the small hotels similarly displayed managerial
weaknesses stemming principally from their backgrounds and
family attitudes to business, but which made it virtually
impossible to extract data for a model comprising attributes
for the forecasting of performance.

Staffing

A similar problem where characteristics could not readily be
gathered for forecasting successful performance concerned
staffing. This emerged as something of a surprise since it
was hypothesised that this was an area that might be
measured for performance purposes. However, in line with
previous findings and the business attitude demeanour of
small firms generally this turned out not to be the case.
    Most of the south Wessex firms (62%) admitted to having
difficulties regarding how many people to employ for optimum
performance. Errors in staffing levels were apparent. The
firms relied too much on occasional signals such as

pressures of work at bottlenecks when the staffing level would probably be adjusted. In yet another area of business management the necessity criterion was in operation. There was also in some cases (28%) seasonal problems where the firms had not calculated the costs of allowing staff to build up or to run down as appropriate. The choice between extra staff or new technology was one avoided by the sample firms.

Recruiting was observed to be regarded as merely advertising for staff, interviewing and selecting. The real costs of recruitment errors where largely unknown and in any event were taken to be acceptable business risks. Some firms were unsure whether they needed new staff or a merit based promotion system. The problem here was the lack of planned training schemes.

All these examples tended to be subjective and incapable of incorporating into models to guide management towards improving performance. Managers differed in their abilities and attitudes when staffing was involved. For example, to achieve any goal of optimisation the sample firms had to set up effective working relationships with employees. Whilst such relationships seemed to work, albeit to varying degrees in the sample firms, these appeared to have been established more by accident or tradition than specific policy.

There were instances where members of a team were not making the best use of their abilities. Some staff expressed disappointment that the jobs they were doing were not the ones they preferred. Managements had not organised work in a structured way. There were occasional examples of managers, in the very small firms mainly, undertaking work that employees should have been doing. They had simply failed to delegate.

All these unpredictable factors raised the question of measuring the performance of staff specifically. The rewarding of performance had the obvious advantage of measuring whether a change had been worthwhile or not. Some work performances that were witnessed were more measurable than others, and the respondent managers emphasised this point. Manual measurement techniques have existed for many years. Unfortunately, about half of the firms were broadly reluctant to adopt management techniques, a finding reinforced in Chapter 4. And even where some attempt at measurement had occurred the staff had not always been involved or even consulted. Management could claim that they had measured performance but the staff were sometimes unaware of it. This posed a serious problem where management had based pay levels on such measurement. Payment on merit schemes derived from performance measurement could only be successful if employees were in agreement. Salary errors could be expensive and some firms had experienced this.

The firms were asked if performance related pay schemes were in operation. About two thirds claimed that performance related pay could only be introduced if the employee could influence his production directly. In reality, there are numerous methods of relating pay to performance but most of the companies were either not fully aware of these or were not interested.

When asked if management would raise salaries for staff where the market rate was higher, most of the firms reluctantly agreed that this would be necessary. However, the market rate would have to 'emerge' before the decision to raise a salary would be implemented. In keeping with most of the 'tests' undertaken throughout the South Wessex Survey management would employ reaction rather than initiation.

Strangely, the subject of trades unions did not enjoy much prominence in these decisions. The vast majority of the south Wessex sample (84%) recognised the unions and most (92%) claimed to pay the union rate. The power of the unions had eased during the 1980's and 1990's and staff pay and conditions were not subject to the prolonged discussions of previous years. A minority of the firms in the 0-24 employee category (8%) claimed not to accept unionisation at all but it was suspected that this was of little consequence given the size of the firm and the nature of its operations.

On the subject of staff motivation the majority response by 78% of the interviewees was that of pay. Yet most agreed that pay could be merely a short run motivation if not related to work effort. Usually, a pay increase was quickly absorbed into normal pay and the beneficial effect, if any, was lost. On the other hand pay was found to be a severe morale reducer when believed to be unfair or low.

There was little doubt that managements were aware of these issues but they tended to ignore obvious possibilities for staff motivation such as where working conditions or requirements were changed too frequently, where management seemed not care about good staff performance, where there was a lack of clear objectives and where staff were treated unfairly.

The measurement of staff performance was a grey zone for South Wessex Survey research purposes where specific characteristics for model building were required. It contrasted notably with the characteristics obtained for the prediction of success and failure of small firms in other areas. It is worth noting that however small a firm is, it nevertheless represents a highly complex and complicated business unit. Models to predict performance might be possible in certain respects but with the majority of observations about small firm behaviour the variables almost inevitably fall into the moulds of the subjective, the qualitative and the unweildy.

Summary

Given the inevitable limitations of such an exercise an effort was made to compile a set of attributes for the forecasting of corporate performance of small business units, although it was not possible to develop the relative successes of both the small and larger firms, and the mechanical and electrical engineering companies in this section of the investigation, not least because of the very small sub-samples that would result. But two groups were identified (those with average returns of 15% or more on capital, and those with less than 15% return) as being successful or unsuccessful. The more successful firms placed less emphasis on consolidation and more on long term growth. Surprisingly, they were less likely to have formal plans and were less likely to identify contribution levels. They were also less likely to use committees to make decisions. The more successful companies were more likely to be market orientated, offer a small range of products, to have a leaner staff and a more intensive appraisal of capital projects. They were more likely to have newer, more productive and higher quality plant and equipment. The results suggested that a small number of managerial factors could possibly predict the financial performances of companies. On the other hand the small hotel provided an interesting contrast to the small engineering firm. The small hotel simply defied the collection of data for the building of a 'forecasting corporate performance' model not least from its lack of organisational structure and managerial and financial discipline. Most of the hotels had persisted with their own methods of operation over the years and had not considered any critical change of approach regarding, for example, staff training, computer installation, enhanced service, external borrowing for investment purposes or advertising. The small hotels' aims were 'family orientated' rather than 'business' and as such the enterprises were operating well below optimum. A similar problem where characteristics could not be readily identified for forecasting successful performance concerned staffing. It was hypothesised that this was an area that might be measurable in performance terms. However, in line with previous findings and the business attitude demeanour of small business units generally this was not the case. The measurement of staff performance was a doubtful field for research purposes where specific characteristics for model building were required. Many of the firms in question believed that staff performance could not be measured since the variables involved were far too subjective and unpredictable.

References

Gillingham, D., Hankinson, A. and Zinger, T. (1987). 'Forecasting Corporate Performance' *British Journal of Canadian Studies*, Vol. 2, No. 1, June.

10   Summary

Introduction

The firms in the South Wessex Survey had concentrated on their main products over the years for various reasons, but tradition as opposed to strategy was a principal explanation. Hardly any of the firms had considered movement into new fields, and diversification was not popular being regarded as risky rather than risk spreading. The impression was that diversification could have been at least as beneficial as the activity currently pursued which was producing sub-optimum results. Firms were allocated a preliminary category according to the degree of production run possible on their main activities. Firms in the specialist production class envied the longer production runs of the long batch production firms who countered by pointing out that 'economies of scale' could be synonymous with lack of innovation and labour monotony. In any event, it seemed likely that certain firms' production run limitations involved them in expense and inconvenience which could possibly have been eased by the pursuance of some relieving policy such as, for example, diversification or market seeking.

In output determination a certain flexibility was essential. Yet nearly half of the sample firms fixed output by allocating quotas that would be retained for some time until events dictated otherwise. Only about one quarter were scheduling output in response to market forces suggesting reasonable degrees of flexibility. But perhaps most striking was another quarter of the sample actually employing constant output policies. Current and expected demand, as measured by the length of order books, were fundamental determinants of output levels, whilst labour availability and excess capacity acted as major influences but no more than that. As far as output constraints were concerned inadequate plant utilisation predominated with rising costs of production, not least the bank interest rates of 1991. Results indicated that very rarely did the firms raise or lower output in the short run in a conscious attempt to optimise sales, profits, costs or overall performance.

It was revealed that the principal goal of about one fifth of the firms was satisfactory profit. Subsidiary policies tended to be rather more individual but two clear aims that repeated themselves were satisfactory or reasonable profits and survival. Key personnel gave specific reasons for adopting their policies. Several claimed that satisfactory profits and survival were the only real goals for small firms, especially during the recessionary conditions of the early 1980's and the early 1990's. However, policies did seem to be the result of historical or traditional behaviour and once a firm had selected a goal this would be retained until events dictated otherwise. Flexibility of policy was not apparent. Indeed, the flexibility normally associated with small firms in general did not match this preconceived notion. From this it seemed clear that a flexible policy could well have increased profits. If profits were not improved then the policy could easily have been changed. Since the firms considered survival either second to satisfactory profits in the hierarchy of objectives or as one of the foundations for profitability, the signs were that the firms were merely aiming to survive. It was possible that survival could have been the fundamental objective since a majority of the firms regarded this as a barometer of success.

Investment

The companies generally agreed that if returns on investment were to be optimised then the application of a specific investment strategy would be necessary. Profit optimality demanded a conscious effort on the part of the decision maker and this would require, among a whole range of techniques and goals, a well defined and implemented investment programme. For example, the emphasis should have been upon vertical investment but 75% of capital expenditure had been basically horizontal. Moreover, even piecemeal investment had tended to be precipitated by crises. There was little evidence of positive investment thinking and very few of the smaller firms admitted to planning ahead beyond twelve months. The majority of the sample firms merely invested when the need arose. In short, most of the investment appeared to be non-strategic, piecemeal, non-anticipatory and geared to survival only.

Whilst there could be little doubt that a recessionary economic situation affected the decision to invest it was equally clear that other, and perhaps more basic, factors were involved. At best, the relationship between investment and the economic climate must be regarded as tenuous. The impression was that investment by many of the firms would have been sub-optimum irrespective of the economic climate, although the rising interest charges imposed by the banks against generally falling base rates during 1991 could not be disregarded. Nevertheless, in most cases individual investment problems could have been tackled more by firm management rather than by reliance upon occasional economic recoveries.

One test of investment effectiveness might be the reponse of capital spending to some important short term development. Whilst several firms could indicate links between labour, output, asset levels, profit, costs, etc., and investment itself, there was little or no evidence to support these relationships over the shorter period despite profit potential. The flexibility normally associated with small firms certainly did not apply significantly to short term capital expenditure and, indeed, the lost opportunities could have been considerable. However, a marked affiliation between real profit in the previous period and real investment in the current period was apparent. This hinted that any government measure that increased post-tax profit directly for the smaller firm would, in turn, stimulate investment.

Having established a relationship between investment and past profits, it would perhaps be misleading to assume that capital spending was determined by this factor alone. There were, of course, instances where investment had been undertaken for reasons other than profit availability. But was this investment active or passive? Was it visionary or merely replacement investment? Unfortunately, investment optimality was undoubtedly likely to be impaired as a result

of non-visionary capital spending by over four fifths of the
sample firms. It was also the case that the mechanical
engineering firms were more guilty of this approach than the
electrical engineering companies. Whilst concrete
conclusions were difficult to reach the general impression
was that investment optimality was falling well short if
only one fifth of the firms had been engaged in visionary
investment. And, of course, there was no guarantee that
even these firms invested positively over the longer term.

Long term investment planning appeared to be an essential
ingredient of strategy if optimality was to be achieved.
Yet very few firms used likely future indicators as specific
influences of their investment decisions. Over half the
sample felt that no reliable indicators existed apart from
historical data.

The findings suggested that capital spending would
probably proceed if the investment item was actually needed,
that the firms' own funds were available, or the cost of
borrowing was not prohibitive in which case the investment
could be postponed. This hardly indicated the pursuit of
investment optimisation. The impression was that investment
was inspired mainly by the necessity criterion which
rendered occasional capital spending imperative. The cost
of borrowing, credit availability and government investment
incentives were all found to be mere influences of
investment only and the authorities were right when they
phased out the latter in the mid-1980's in favour of lower
corporation tax.

Finance

In the South Wessex Survey the majority of the firms had
used banking facilities for investment purposes only when
their own, or private funds, had been inadequate. Some
firms had obtained funds from their parent company or group
but whether this, in turn, had been provided externally was
difficult to establish. It was reasonably certain that a
large part of the firms' long term finances for investment
had been provided by owners' capital, past profits and
private loans. Bank support for capital ventures (as opposed
to overdraft facilities) was seemingly a reluctant last
resort. Without doubt the firms preferred to use their own
funds for investment purposes and, indeed, some companies
had adopted a specific non-borrowing policy. Additionally,
there was no shortage of external finance during normal
market conditions but it was very soon in evidence that the
south Wessex firms did not, in the main, resort to these
funds. In fact, the impression was that institutional

finance was to be avoided and an outstanding feature of the
evidence was that over 90% of the sample had not been
concerned in any attempt to obtain investment finance
through facilities beyond the local bank or other subsidiary
source. Several companies actually outlined opportunities
for expansion and improvement but still preferred the status
quo. Some visionary investment via the institutions,
despite occasionally high interest charges, could well have
taken advantage of the very opportunities identified by the
firms themselves. There was no doubt that the institutions
ensured that a venture would be basically profitable before
funds were made available and therefore the inference was
that profits were being lost by the firms' refusals to
resort to these funds. In other words, the companies in
question appeared to be content with an investment finance
situation that could conceivably have contributed to sub-
optimum investment levels and sub-optimum investment
returns.

Nearly one third of the sample was convinced that lack of
government intervention, e.g. to control recessionary
conditions, was the reason for low investment in the small
firm sector. Taxation figured fairly prominently as an
adverse influence on investment finance decisions,
especially up to the mid-1980's, in that likely funds were
being taxed away indiscriminately. An interesting aspect of
the findings was that nearly one quarter of the firms
believed that governments practised anti-small firm policies
because very few real, positive and direct incentives were
available. Too many of the firms were simply not aware of
the numerous measures across the spectrum introduced by the
government between 1980 and 1991. But what exactly did
small firms expect from governments? An ambivalent attitude
could be discerned in that on the one hand firms had
repeatedly valued their independent decision making
capability whilst on the other they clearly expected some
kind of assistance from the authorities. A significant
tenth of the sample reinforced the need for a restoration of
confidence by the curbing of inflation long term. A growing
number of respondents required mandatory lower borrowing
rates. About 15% wanted taxation to be even lower than the
1991 level, and some called for its abolition in favour of
the ploughing back of profits into investment channels. And
another tenth suggested more government direct contracts for
small firms. It was observed that small companies'
investment was more likely to respond to government action
that impacted directly on profitability rather than to
policy that produced indirect, delayed or unidentifiable
financial assistance.

The period 1970-1982 was historically an interesting one
in research terms for it contained wide degrees of

government credit control. In 1970 the original monetary policy rules were in force including 'stop-go'. By the end of 1971 the rules were reversed and credit availability via the 'Competition and Credit Controls' policy was in operation and expansion continued throughout 1972. However, a tightening up of the system could be discerned during 1973. The beginning of a return to the old controls emerged during 1974 and by early 1975 the full circle was virtually complete. In the late 1970's monetarism, unemployment, recession and inflation had all operated whilst in the early 1980's the posting of the minimum lending rate had been abolished along with the banks' 12½% reserve asset ratio. Thus, some of the South Wessex Survey firms had experienced control and then market freedom, not to mention uncertainty, in at least two governmental phases since 1970. Incidentally, even if a case could be made in defence of the banks the fact remained that over 90% of the sample firms were dissatisfied in some way, if not totally, with the services offered by the banks between 1970 and 1991. But essentially, the findings showed that credt availability had had little or no effect on three quarters of the sample, and where some influence was apparent this had occurred only under special conditions. If finance were made available then this in itself would be no determinant of investment and thus the picture indicated that if governments wished to stimulate investment in small firms then the implementation of various credit policies should, on the face of it, be awarded low priority. Firms had simply invested as required and had not taken advantage of easy credit facilities when available. Moreover, in support of this, assuming that the real money supply was both a reasonable indication of monetary expansion and the growth of funds intended for capital expenditure, the relationship between the money supply and south Wessex investment was nominal only. In general terms during the period under review investment by the sample firms appeared not to have been influenced unduly by government credit control aspirations.

With high interest rates prevailing, for example, in the early 1990's, would a persistently low bank base rate actually stimulate investment by small firms? The responses indicated that, given the inevitable time lags, a rising cost of borrowing would reduce capital expenditure by small firms far more than a falling cost of borrowing would increase it. Many firms in the south Wessex sample felt that the old minimum lending rate (or the current base rate) had had little impact on investment decisions generally, and considered that the relationship between base rates and investment was indeterminate at best. However, it was possible, although not without some difficulty, to observe isolated instances in the sample firms when investment

seemed have been responsive to changes in the rate of
interest:

Where a capital project might have had yields that
stetched far into the future
Where a firm was already working to tight margins
and there was not the scope for increasing prices
through market imperfections
Where a shortage of internal funds might have necessitated
greater reliance on external borrowing
Where interest charges on stocks might have represented a
higher percentage of total cost in certain small firms

Alternatively:

Investment would remain constant if the rate change was
marginal only, if the project was vital and if future
yields were not too unpredictable
Investment would fall if the rate rose significantly from
any level, if the project was not vital and if the
outlay was large
Investment would rise if the rate fell significantly, if
the lower rate persisted longer term, if future yields
were predictable and if the project was re-defined as
vital

But certainly the investment behaviour of the south Wessex
firms with regard to the cost of borrowing appeared to be
somewhat involved and unpredictable and one could only infer
that monetary poloicy involving nominal changes in the rate
of interest to influence investment had not enjoyed, and was
unlikely to enjoy, notable measures of success.
    Since 1979 investment incentives had been available and
consistently improved. Yet only a very small minority of
the firms could claim that these incentives had had any
influence on their capital expenditure decisions.   And
although about half of the companies said that their
investment plans might be encouraged by incentives they,
nevertheless, regarded this influence as insignificant. The
investment decisions of 44% of the sample had clearly not
been affected in any way by government investment aids. The
majority of the companies were obviously only interested in
incentives when these actually coincided with their own
plans for investment. If firms were investment optimising
then presumably they would be aid optimising also, but this
was patently not the case. As a consequence it was hardly
possible that the firms in question were optimising their
investment returns as far as incentives were concerned.
Indeed, the vast majority of the sample was unware of the
many incentives available. It must be reiterated that the

phasing out of investment tax allowances by the government
in the mid-1980's for lower taxation was probably long
overdue.

Appraisal

The South Wessex Survey data indicated that the payback and
rate of return methods of investment appraisal were by far
the most popular used. Some 44% of the firms employed these
traditional, and suspect, approaches. Only 8% used
discounted cash flow, whilst nearly half the firms in the
sample used trial and error methods or none at all. Of the
50 firms in the full population no firm was totally familiar
with the pitfalls of discounted cash flow. Firms that did
use some method of appraisal were not always clear how or
why the technique had been selected or adopted in the first
instance, and over 40% claimed their method to be of
traditional origin. Practically no firm had been influenced
by the literature on the subject. Advanced forecasting of
cash flows was not in evidence and almost one third used no
method whatsoever. Just over 10% made attempts to assess
cash flow on a calculated basis. Over three quarters of the
sample using traditional methods or no method at all
admitted to no major amendments in system or policy. In
general terms the firms in question did not present an
encouraging picture in respect of the selection, employment,
flexibility of approach and potential improvement of the
investment appraisal method. The firms' attitudes tended to
fall into two camps: firms using the traditional methods
believed that the quality of the investment appraisal
decision was not influenced too much by the quality of the
investment appraisal method, whilst firms employing the more
modern techniques conceded, with reservations, that the
quality of the method could possibly enhance the quality of
the decision and the ultimate return on capital. On balance
considering the available evidence it was almost certain
that levels of investment and rates of return, even if
acceptable to the firms in their own estimation, were
inconsistent with any goal of optimality as a result of most
firms being unfamiliar with the techniques of investment
appraisal.
The respondents were asked to indicate the most important
management techniques employed including investment
appraisal. Budgeting in its widest sense appeared to be the
most popular but nearly half of the firms could not indicate
a major operations research or management technique method
at all, and only one firm recorded investment appraisal,
i.e. discounted cash flow, as a management aid. However,

two main problems persisted. Firstly, it was not easy to categorise specifically the firms that were employing some management techniques, and those that were clearly using none. Every firm could show to varying degrees that certain 'systems' and 'methods' were in operation. And secondly, in some instances the introduction of sophisticated operations research techniques would be fairly difficult, if not impossible for some of the smaller firms.

The firms employing the traditional methods generally presented incomplete and inadequate appraisals. On the other hand, the companies using discounted cash flow produced better evaluations but, even so, were not immune from criticism. Overall, the investment appraisals and investment strategies practised were, again, at odds with the goal of optimisation. For example, the most popular combination of factors taken into account was taxation, incentives and inflation. Nevertheless, only about one quarter of the sample acknowledged these with depreciation surprisingly not listed. Less than 10% felt the need to make adjustments for inflation. And a point of some interest was that no firm considered that such items as risk, uncertainty, obsolescence and opportunity cost could be practically catered for. Undoubtedly, the approach to the method and the variables to be included inclined far more towards the trial and error than the mathematical. Whether or not some factors were self-correcting, self-cancelling or simply non-measurable remained arguable but, in any event, would be no substitute for rigour. Similarly, although certain types of investment could indeed overshadow the calculations, and the final accounts could automatically reflect net returns long term, this tended simply to confirm the rule of thumb attitude rather than defend it.

Profitability

The target rate of return on net assets and the mark-up on costs are mathematically related. But the south Wessex firms that, in the main, failed to reach their own set targets could hardly have done otherwise with the mark-ups employed. Even allowing for adverse market conditions when shortfalls were perhaps inevitable for some companies it remained true that the majority were simply not co-ordinating the mark-up with the required target rate of return. For many firms the relationship between mark-up and target was presumably unknown, and the evidence suggested that the problem lay more within the pricing rather than with the setting up of the target rate of return by the firm in the first instance.

The severe difficulties in actually measuring a company's performance were acknowledged at the outset, but since the majority of the south Wessex firms expressed their profitability in terms of a 'rate of return on net assets' this particular criterion was adopted. It was soon evident that policies of rigid targeting, which exemplified a behavioural pattern closely allied to survival, were generally employed by the sample firms. Moreover, the minimum acceptable rate of return tended to be determined by specific circumstances or events, and any apparent flexibility was directed more towards horizontal rather than vertical investment. Whilst several firms had exceeded their expectations, even during the recessionary conditions of early 1991, many had not reached their targets, others had failed to achieve even the minimum aspiration and some had sustained losses. Too many of the firms actually failed to reach the very targets they had set themselves. Reasons for this failure rate were not hard to identify for the sample as a whole, and these have already been presented earlier. But the major reason given by the firms for the failure to reach target returns on net assets was 'uncontrollable external factors', and only 14% considered that their own inadequate investment strategies, expertise and appraisals might have caused financial performance to be below par. Only a minority felt that a more positive investment approach was required and many believed that no action could be taken to raise profitability significantly owing to outside constraints. No firm could guarantee that any consultancy recommendation put forward to improve returns would, in fact, be implemented.

On this particular topic a highly significant four fifths of the south Wessex sample firms had neither employed, nor had considered employing, outside expertise, believing consultants to be unnecessary, over-rated, expensive, inventors of problems, disruptive and representative of external interference. But two other studies, mentioned in Chapter 5, showed that the firms in those samples were highly satisfied, in the main, with the consultancy received. It seemed reasonable to conclude that the south Wessex firms' strong reservations about consultancy were very much over-stated and outside expertise could well have aided the pursuit of the profitability so obviously lacking.

With regard to the mechanical and electrical engineering firms in the sample, at a time of recession the former had not responded to the need for investment beyond the level of repairs and maintenance. These companies were more concerned about survival than the electrical engineering units. They relied upon the necessity criterion more, they had not taken advantage of the incentives available, they used fewer management techniques and they were less ready to admit their deficiencies. However, it was likely that the electrical engineering industry, that appeared to stand up to the tests of strategy, finance, appraisal and profitability better than the mechanical engineering sector, had been encouraged to invest in new technology by the rapidly changing nature of a demanding market.

There was also a suspicion of evidence that the specialist one-off producers performed better than the batch producers, especially during adverse economic conditions. This was probably the result of the demands of being in a specialist field where contracts had to be individually calculated against competition, and investment equipment obtained specially in order to undertake the work accepted.

Pricing

The literature on pricing was somewhat inconsistent and contradictory. A contribution to this area, especially in relation to the small firm, was an aim of the South Wessex Survey. Examples of these inconsistencies in pricing literature are contained in Chapter 6. These comprised findings such as:

Firms were vague about the mechanics of marginalism and relied instead upon full cost pricing
Marginalism was strongly implanted in pricing behaviour.
Firms were less interested in profit maximisation than in secure incomes
Firms based price upon total cost
Cost plus percentage pricing was very much influenced by competition and demand
Firms making the distinction between fixed and variable costs were, in essence, employing marginalism
Full cost pricing was well established but there were many marginalist and behavioural qualifications
Price was a crucial element in explaining consumer behaviour
There was a strong relationship between sales and price
Business management did not agree with the economic views of the importance of pricing
Price acted as an indicator of quality
The size of the mark-up on cost and the level of planned investment were related
Pricing had been ruled by hit or miss instinct but was now more objective and systematic
The main problems in pricing were not problems of principle but empirical ones in that pricing was based upon information, and information collection was

invariably of doubtful quality

Not surprisingly, contributors and students have felt
uncertain about the various pricing studies available. And
material in relation to small firm pricing in the real world
is particularly lacking.

On the available evidence all firms in the south Wessex
sample made cost the essence of price calculation, but a
minority claimed that non-cost pricing was practised on
necessary occasions. Costs had to be covered in the first
instance but the ultimate selling price would be determined
by what the market would bear at the relevant output level,
or the price set by competitors. Where this ultimate price
exceeded cost it would be applied over the longer term;
where it fell below cost it would be regarded as a short run
venture only. This was, of course, indicative of flexible
mark-ups. The effect of rival prices was not strong, unless
forced upon the firm by minor crisis. Most firms adopted
the full cost approach to pricing. There was little
evidence of price being determined by marginalist and
behavioural qualifications. Rivalry and demand influences
were also somewhat weak. An estimated four fifths of the
firms employed a cost based price. It would seem remarkable
that the majority should opt for this method when its
limitations were severe. The distinction between price
determinants and price influences must be stressed. Cost
was the major determinant but market conditions were
regarded merely as influences by the respondents. But even
if firms practised more flexible pricing when observing
these externalities, this policy appeared to be more imposed
by the nature of the market rather than by conscious
strategy. It was possible that this distinction between
determinants and influences might go some way towards
explaining the occasional conflict in the literature.

The south Wessex data gave the clear impression that
pricing tended to be rigid, but the pricing of one-off jobs
was considerably more flexible. What the market would pay
figured far more prominently in the calculation of one-off
pricing than for routine batch production. Flexible pricing
was possible, it was practised, it was profitable and
successful, but virtually exclusively on one-off contracts.

Closely allied to full cost pricing is pricing in order to
achieve a target rate of return on investment. In effect,
firms pursuing this target return do so by calculating a
mark-up on full costs according to the harmonisation of
mark-up and target by the well known formula touched on in
Chapter 6. The sample firms, in the main, adopted a
targeting approach. Unfortunately, there was little, or no,
evidence of the required mathematical harmony between the
mark-up and the target rate of return. Even if the mark-ups

were initially correct firms tended not to adjust prices on a continual basis. The mark-up soon became obsolete to achieve the target. Firms failing to reach their own targets could hardly have done otherwise with the mark-ups employed. Price rigidity might have maintained customer relations but it had also hindered financial performance. Was the target set too high, or was the mark-up set too low? It can only be stated that the firms set their targets largely by convention and no doubt based upon what they considered to be reasonably attainable. The most frequently mentioned rationalisation included: 'fair and reasonable return', 'the traditional industry concept of a fair return' and 'the desire to equal or better the firm's average return over a recent period of time'. One might conclude from this, and also because of the preference for price stability among the south Wessex firms, that the problem of failing to reach expected targets lay more within the pricing rather than the targeting.

In adopting cost plus pricing one drawback of this method rested on the assumption that firms actually knew what their costs of production were at given levels of output. It was by no means certain that the sample firms did have such information to hand. And even where costs had been monitored and analysed the problem of adjusting prices for inflation was an interesting one. Customers were generally reluctant to pay current prices under recessionary economic conditions and the firms preferred to hold prices rather than adjust for inflation on a continual basis. This was especially the case during 1990 and early 1991. Prices should be adjusted by small amounts and often and not held constant for twelve months as a policy. The sample firms were clearly unaware of the rapid erosion of profits by delayed price adjustments for increased costs of production and for inflation in particular. Some interviewees felt that when inflation was at 5% this had been manageable. The problem was that many firms used materials that had risen in price by far greater amounts than 5% yet still believed that inflation was 'self-correcting'.

There was a low level of basic cost awareness. Too many firms were without any policy at all for cost monitoring or cost economising. Some companies simply assumed that their costs were already at a minimum. Many firms believed that the 'recession' was responsible for disappointing results. Moreover, contribution analysis was conspicuous by its relative absence. The importance of this technique cannot be over-emphasised yet respondents seemed committed to absorption rather than contribution costing.

Despite the controversy regarding the importance of price in the literature it has usually been accepted that price and customer demand are inversely related. But the survey data revealed that whilst a significant raising of price by the firms would certainly contract demand, a marginal increase would not. Similarly, a marked lowering of price would extend demand but a nominal decrease would not. Thus, the demand curve clearly possessed a vertical section at the relevant output level. The firms themselves admitted that price could be raised and no sales would be lost. Why did the firms not take advantage of this? Obviously, all firms would have to resort to price adjustments in order to counter inflation from time to time, but it appeared that very few were prepared to raise price to the point that they themselves knew to be more profitable than any other. Firms simply fixed price by the conventional cost plus percentage method but below the upper limit of the vertical section of the demand curve.

Only a few firms were pursuing short run markets via pricing flexibility. It could be the case that small firms in persisting with the goal of survival do not have the will or the vision to apply pricing and market flexibility. The literature, despite its limitations, does show that managerial aims and strategies, not least in the pricing field, can be for flexibility. Pricing was too often treated as a technical problem to be solved by applying rules or procedures and not as a creative marketing challenge to be met with a new insight into buyers' motivations.

The relationship between pricing and investment is thought to exist in some firms, albeit large ones. No such relationship appeared to exist in the Wessex firms. They, again, invested when the need arose rather than for strategic purposes. If prices were affected by an investment decision then this would tend to be coincidental. Capital expenditure presented a quite separate problem from pricing as outlined in previous chapters.

Could the respondents themselves suggest what might be done to make pricing more efficient? Only a small minority had considered the issues sufficiently to conclude that a more positive pricing approach was essential. An even more remarkable, and disappointing, feature was the significant number that believed no action could be taken since activities were severely constrained by external market forces beyond control. Another statistic of interest was the few having agreed that certain actions were possible to improve pricing, then stated that the likelihood of these measures actually being implemented was remote. The suggestion that advisory services might help in such circumstances raised the whole question of consultancy once again.

It was found that some firms had resorted to outside expertise such as accountants, bank managers, the advisory

145

services, etc., but not specifically for pricing purposes. Others felt that external assistance might be useful and would consider it but only if the need arose. A large majority had neither employed nor had considered employing consultants for pricing advice. Generally, the interviewees believed that management consultants were just not required by small firms. They were described, again, as over-rated, expensive and disruptive. The chances were that the Wessex firms' pricing could have been employed more purposefully with the occasional help of consultants than without them.

During recessionary conditions it was understandable that future uncertainty could affect pricing. It was also clear that other, and perhaps more basic factors, were relevant. The impression was that the pricing expertise of many of the firms would have been sub-standard in any event. Firms complained that because of the recession in the early 1990's customers would only pay last year's prices. On the other hand, the south Wessex firms apparently had no choice other than to pay current prices for supplies. This situation was regarded as an external problem beyond the control of the sample firms. Although it could be argued that certain market difficulties were indeed outside the firms' sphere of influence, this particular pricing problem did seem to be yet another self-imposed barrier. There was very little diversification, expertise and service were insufficiently exploited and full cost pricing was the norm.

The firms were asked to identify the most important area of assistance that the government might implement to make pricing decisions easier for small firms. An ambivalent attitude could be sensed in that on the one hand the firms defended their need for independence from government intervention, whilst on the other they obviously wanted assistance of some kind from the authorities. But this required assistance did not include indirect aid. Direct help was expected. Unfortunately, very few of the firms had any specific recommendations to make regarding pricing. Indeed, the sample firms were very largely unaware of the actual assistance on offer by government between 1980 and 1991.

Given the make-up of the sample with two thirds in mechanical engineering and one third in electrical engineering, the various tests revealed that approaches to pricing by the latter were relatively superior to the former's. One might suspect that electrical engineering companies throughout the 1980's and early 1990's were being extended by the nature of a demanding progressive market, where as such rapid change was not apparent for the traditional jobbing mechanical engineering firms. Nevertheless, the electrical engineering units did emerge with the rather better overall record of pricing expertise.

Almost half the firms were entrenched in a survival mentality to varying degrees and this could be observed in the firms' conceptions of price determination, one-off jobs, mark-ups, inflation, costs of production, market demand, price flexibility, investment, pricing improvement, the economic climate, consultancy and government involvement.

Output

When investigating the goals of the south Wessex firms, sales revenue optimisation was a reasonable, if not prominent, alternative to survival. It was surprising, however, that sales volume optimisation was not. In this regard some of the literature examined in Chapter 7 showed that:

Output maximisation was the basic objective behind typical Soviet enterprises

Output maximisation with a profit contraint could fit the motives of some private firms, and also of those public services which were judged by their breaking even whilst preferably raising output or service at the same time

Product line strategy was one of the most important areas in market strategy

If a firm sets quantity then price was uncertain; if a firm sets price then quantity was uncertain

Output decisions, price decisions and investment decisions were highly interdependent

Inputs, prices and outputs were all affected by demand uncertainty and rigorous demand forecasting by firms was essential

Raw material ordering decisions in small firms were very much restricted by external forces

Just how far output optimisation for small firms could be developed remained something of an unknown factor.

The ultimate effectiveness of the typical south Wessex firm was its ability to attract a continous flow of new orders. Three major factors were likely to influence this inflow: price, delivery and advertising communication. Efficient operation of any system also required a minimum level of work in progress to ensure that when a particular resource finished a task another job was waiting to start. All this was accepted by the south Wessex firms but what was much less well appreciated was that overfilling the system was potentially just as damaging as underfilling it. Balanced scheduling was required but perfect matching was impossible because both the volume and the work content of the input were always dynamic. The point was that in some firms imbalance appeared to be an integral part of the process. The cost of meeting peak loads at different points in the system was vital but the majority of the firms did not give this much priority. Successful output determination by the sample firms required more thought than simply allocating fixed quotas of work to departments, sections and individuals. A certain flexibility was needed to avoid obvious pitfalls, but this required degree of flair was singularly absent among many of the firms. The typical unit waited for a contract to arrive and then allocated output quotas subject to certain plant constraints Three broad approaches to output determination could be discerned: output levels geared specifically to market demand, output levels fixed on a target or quota per period system and output levels held constant as a policy. Only one quarter of the firms were scheduling output in response to market forces implying reasonable degrees of flexibility. About half of the firms fixed output simply by allocating quotas which would be retained until events dictated otherwise. But even more striking was the finding that the remaining quarter actually employed a 'constant output' policy. Whilst it is certainly not claimed that output manipulation alone will produce the highest attainable profits, it is suggested that firms displaying a marked inflexibility of output manipulation would be unlikely to optimise returns on capital.

Current and expected demand, as measured by the length of order books, were patently regarded as the fundamental determinants of output levels by all firms, but output influences added some complexity. For example, after output levels had been fixed it sometimes became necessary to adjust the targets set, possibly as a result of unpredictable labour shortages. These short run factors were regarded not as determinants but as subsidiary influences of output levels. Even so, the results plainly indicated that very rarely did the firms raise or lower output in a conscious attempt to improve sales, profits or even costs.

As far as the South Wessex Survey was concerned three questions were important in the assessment of output efficiency. What was the average level of excess capacity? What was the extent of product development, demand estimation, advertising, product development and exporting? And particularly if outputs were raised to full capacity what would happen to costs, prices and profits? Maximum excess capacity had to be estimated by the firms and was inevitably presented as an average over time. But care was taken to ensure that the figures quoted were indicative of the extra output the firm could produce without recourse to overtime working, excessive demands on machinery or management, etc. Practically every firm in the sample had experienced some degree of excess capacity between 1980 and 1991 and occasionally these unused resources had amounted to 50% and over. No firm could claim continuous zero excess capacity but it is worth pointing out that generally speaking it was the specialist one-off production electrical engineering firms that tended to perform better than those engaged in mechanical engineering work. Incidentally, the decision to accept subsidiary work was not always based upon the profitable elimination of excess capacity. The situation was that spare output facility was available. Firms themselves admitted that if production could be raised to the 100% level then unit costs and possibly prices could be reduced involving the firm in no apparent financial hardship. Spare capacity would have been profitable to eliminate, but the firms were far too slow to take advantage of the opportunities to hand.

The response from the firms that full capacity working would be readily undertaken if contracts were available was not necessarily a valid point for a competitive firm to make. For instance, to what extent did firms actually seek out new possibilities and move into and out of reasonably accessible markets? The finding was that very few interviewees could confirm that this was done as a specific policy of the firm, although many considered that market seeking could be a profitable venture. What was the level of product development, advertising, demand estimation and exporting? It has already been highlighted in Chapter 8 that a low priority was accorded to 'marketing', which in turn affected the output determination decision. One could not describe the firms as market conscious although the interviewees thought they were. Most respondents considered that product development, market research and demand forecasting could have led to increased outputs and profits (and reduced excess capacity) but the majority simply did not practise these activities. Advertising was distinguishable only by its relative obscurity. It was strongly felt that small firms did not need to advertise. The reliance upon local reputation was a rather doubtful substitute. Additionally, since a number of the firms did not actually have a product they considered product development an irrelevance. They overlooked their unique features such as quality work, servicing, deliveries on time, personal service, etc. Too few had exploited these undoubted qualities. It might be concluded that the output problems of small firms could almost certainly have been eased, if not solved, by the application of the basic marketing and output skills impliedly lacking in the findings.

As far as output constraints were concerned, inadequate relevant plant capacity predominated. Generally, four questions had to be answered before the south Wessex firms could proceed with output activity. Could the product actually be made? Was labour, plant, machinery and expertise available? Was finance, preferably the firm's own, to hand? And was the relevant capacity right? These constituted the major constraints on output levels. The inevitable recessionary economic climate was also regarded as an output constraint beyond the control of the firms. Contracts normally placed by larger companies, government departments, overseas firms, etc., had not materialised from time to time during 1980 to 1991, and in some cases larger firms had themselves taken on the work normally done by smaller units. Government cuts were especially singled out as reasons for below capacity working. A quite different set of constraints apparently prevented exporting, an issue given some prominence in Chapter 8. Home markets were generally preferred to those abroad where it was claimed currency problems, language difficulties, legal hindrances and uncertainty of payment prevented long term selling overseas. Yet some firms in the sample had been able to by-pass the recession by occasional purposeful market seeking which in some cases had included expanding output for export outlets.

What were the sample firms' overall investment strategies with particular reference to output determination? Most interviewees confirmed earlier findings by insisting that investment was based upon the necessity criterion. This usually involved having the firm's own finance available (if possible), the hurried establishment of equipment need and the absence of recognised investment appraisal techniques. There were, in the main, no rigorous links between capital spending and output planning. Firms obviously expected newly installed equipment to produce better quality work, to speed up production, to eliminate waste and to improve the working conditions for labour. But there was little actual evidence that these factors were quantified in more than a superficial way.

Output techniques such as production scheduling, stock control, quality control, not to mention total quality management, just in time, direct line feed, etc., can be adapted to be used in most firms and can improve financial performance. However, once again, it appeared that the majority of the Wessex firms did not take advantage of these techniques. Perhaps they looked too much to rapid financial improvement when results were not realised in an immediately visible form. There seemed to be the well known problem of lack of awareness in this respect. Overall, it was found

that half the sample employed no observable output
techniques at all. In some cases firms admitted that
certain techniques were applicable but these had not been
considered over the 1980 to 1991 period under review. A
minority were using quality control, production
'scheduling', critical path analysis, work study, etc., but
to what extent these were effectively employed was difficult
to judge. It was true that some companies felt, for
example, that critical path analysis was impracticable in
their particular situations but, even so, this could not
excuse the absence of this, and other techniques, if
suppliers and customers employed it. A few interviewees
volunteered that although some output techniques could have
been profitably applied, they had never been introduced and
no sound reasons for this were offered. A few suggested
that output techniques in general could actually mislead
decisions. Yet the use of output techniques in industry
across the spectrum has been increasing over the years and
it appears that more and more work is being carried out in
the field of evaluating the outcomes of these techniques
which may further improve the methods and encourage more
small firms to make full use of them.

Only 14% of the Wessex sample had employed consultants for
output determination improvement. A few more companies had
engaged consultants for reasons other than output purposes,
but the fact remained that nearly three quarters of the
firms had never used consultants.

The south Wessex sample firms were categorised in terms of
employees in the groups 0-24 and 25-100. In examining such
areas as output determinants, the economic climate, excess
capacity, output rigidity, marketing, investment, output
techniques and the government aid, no significant
correlations emerged between 'performance' in the above
areas and the size of firm, except where stated
occasionally. All firms seemed to be in need of
improvement.

A similar situation existed with the production run
categories of the one-off specialist and the batch producer.
Apart from the fact that the former did tend to be in a
slightly stronger position under adverse conditions, there
were no obvious links between the production categories and
the firms' industrial track records.

Moreover, the South Wessex Survey in revealing endemic
problems of output determination, indicated that the
electrical engineering firms emerged with some credit from
the various 'tests'. Unquestionably stimulated by the
nature of a progressive market they demonstrated a notable
reposnse to these challenges. The mechanical engineering
jobbers were somewhat less so inclined.

Finally, it must be emphasised, not for the first time,

that most firms seemed pre-occupied with survival when alternative philosophies of operation were open to them. Survival, of course, can be positive in that a firm may strive for ultra efficiency to survive a take-over bid. Unfortunately, the survival in terms of the south Wessex firms over the period 1980 to 1991 was clearly of a negative characteristic.

The results indicated that the firms' output determination was demonstrably inconsistent with the goal of optimisation. The firms under review appeared to brush aside, and even ignore, openings for improved performance via more effective output management. As a consequence of these non-rigorous attitudes returns on capital were inevitably below those reasonably attainable.

Marketing

Only one tenth of the south Wessex sample pursued sales expansion as an objective but 38% had no marketing policies at all. There was a heavy reliance upon repeat orders, maintenance of local reputation and, not least, product quality. But overall it was mainly a question of ad hoc marketing in response to current demand. Policies, if they existed, were reactive to events, a situation very much in line with findings presented in previous chapters.

Some 40% of the firms employed no qualified marketing staff. Indeed, very few staff had marketing backgrounds. Only 6% of the firms had marketing departments.

The firms' attempts to overcome the lack of skilled labour problems, and especially in marketing, fell far short of formal training. Day release was the main outlet for the technical and technologist grades, whilst short course attendance was a significant method for managerial and clerical staff.

Several firms pointed out that to train labour only to see it competed away by the larger firms could be both expensive and frustrating for the small company. In essence, what was on offer was basic 'on the job' or 'hands on' training rather than a well planned inductive and systematic training programme. The very small firms in the sample saw training as, again, a cost and not as an investment. This attitude could not, of course, substitute for the rigorous on-going training urgently required for the 1990's and beyond.

By their own admissions 16% of the firms had no training at all. No firm had employed consultants to advise on training. In-house seminars were few and far between. Of the training topics that had been pursued computing and health and safety were the most prominent. Management of change, Just in Time and notably marketing were low down on the list. No firms in the entire 50 firm sample had asked staff to attend courses or conferences specifically on '1992'.

On the other hand, some staff regarded courses as a 'break from work'. Others were not always enthusiastic about training despite its 'time off' appeal. The South Wessex Survey confirmed that labour was regarded by the firms as the most valuable asset. Effective training could only have enhanced that asset but the firms casually rejected the challenge.

The encouragement of small firms has been something of a priority of government assistance during 1980-1991. To some extent this has been seen as a means of easing the problems of unemployment. However, there has been insufficent knowledge as to whether small firms create jobs or not. There has also been a lack of data regarding the types of jobs small firms create. A number of questions were put to the firms in an attempt to probe into this area.

Of the firms involved there was no one size of firm responsible for the majority of jobs created. In fact, there was little job creation overall not least because of the small firm's inability to attract skilled labour, including marketing staff. Very few new jobs had been created and half were estimated to be re-located ones in any event. Again, of the jobs created about half had been offset by staff resignations. It was unlikely that the firms would create new jobs in the marketing area given these facts. No firm could claim that jobs had been created to prepare for future developments. All firms invested in labour as and when the need arose.

Only 50% of the sample practised market research albeit to varying and suspect standards. Many regarded forecasting as 'impossible' given the periodic recessionary conditions during the 1980's and 1990's. Only 6% were engaged in purposeful and continuous market research. Most firms claimed that the local market was known. There was no need to research it.

Regarding product development, only 16% were engaged in identifiable new product and part product development. Much of the observable product development comprised a reaction to need. And whilst the firms felt that there was a shortage of external funds for product development in the U.K., previous findings have shown that the firms had a marked reluctance to use external finance if it could possibly be avoided. Product development expertise existed in most of the firms but the distinct lack of product development tended to expose, once again, lost opportunities.

There was some uncertainty regarding the difficulties of

selling new products. Very few firms had entered the product development arena yet felt that there must be severe problems at the selling stage. Had more product development been undertaken it was possible that the experience gained might have made product development expectations not only more realistic but also more likely to be realised.

Product development was recognised as essential for progress by the firms but some respondents with fewer opportunities for product development tended to dismiss it. The alternatives of developing service, speeding up delivery, etc., had not been given serious consideration. The product development potential far exceeded its likely implementation.

The firms were invited to explain their advertising policies. Nearly 60% of the sample had no advertising approaches that could be regarded as effective. Of the firms that did advertise a number claimed that responses to their efforts over the period 1980-1991 had been disappointing. Almost 90% of the sample had apparently not analysed the effectiveness of any advertsing undertaken.

It was considered by some companies that small firms did not need to advertise. In reality, there was no shortage of relevant advertising outlets for the small business, and no shortage either of local consultants to advise, but whilst these advertising possibilities generated some interest with the interviewees there was, in the end, a minimal interest in the pursuit of them.

Only 4% of the firms were exporting over 20% of their total output. The bottom line was that nearly 70% had not sold abroad throughout the time the firm in question had been in existence. Generally speaking, it was the larger firms that were more export minded although from a low base.

Why should the export records of the south Wessex firms be so poor? The main reason for this was that the firms believed that exporting was bedevilled by pitfalls including legal requirements, currency complications and language barriers. The sheer effort needed for successful exporting was not considered to be worthwhile. Too many of the firms had rejected exporting and especially since excess capacities could have been eased by prudent selling abroad.

The familiar story again unfolded with regard to export consultants. Only 3 of the firms out of the 50 had engaged consultants for export purposes. For successful exporting to occur the firm had to follow a critical path through the map of opportunities. The advice centres could readily assist with guidelines, but most firms had not even approached the export services for preliminary soundings. With 1992 looming the position was not encouraging.

Had the firms adapted information technology to their marketing practices? Whilst 70% had a computer installed its main use was for word processing rather than for specific marketing purposes. The most popular reason for installation was to save time, the least popular reason was to be more accurate. Nearly 90% of the firms thought that a computer system to cover just the marketing function would be simply too costly.

Almost 70% had recently upgraded their hardware. The remainder had not, although some of these had only recently purchased their computers. There were examples, however, of a minority of firms that had purchased computers some years ago and had not upgraded and had no intention of doing so within the foreseeable future.

Of the firms that actually owned computers thirteen (37%) claimed not to have had any major problems with their software packages. But 17% felt that training had been a difficulty. Given the small firm's general attitude towards training this finding came as no surprise. And no surpise either to learn that 19 out of the 35 firms admitted to some disruption during the implementation of the technology into the workplace.

Whether for use in the marketing context or otherwise it did seem that some of the firms with computers had purchased equipment they did not really need. It raised the point that in some cases a good manual system would have been the better investment.

Why do firms engage in marketing partnership practices? There could be several sound reasons for this, not least to share expertise and to share risks. In the south Wessex sample only 4 firms were able to demonstrate an attempt, if not more than that, at informal partnership with larger purchasers and suppliers. In some instances this partnership was almost a necessary imposition. Inbound and outbound logistics had not been communicated in any way to purchasers and suppliers by the vast majority of the sample firms. They, in turn, had not requested purchasers or suppliers to advise them. Suppliers had not been researched despite occasional questionable service during the 1980-1991 period. Five firms admitted, however, that certain large major purchasers had researched them.

The firms suggested that partnership barriers existed and pricing was a good example. Apparently, one could negotiate in a partnership situation freely on design, quality and delivery, but much less on price.

There was little evidence of the firms offering subsidies to assist suppliers to meet requirements. Contracts, once placed, were left to the supplier to implement and deliver. Similarly, the sample companies had not investigated how they might integrate their own systems and procedures in partnership believing that purchasers and suppliers would probably not co-operate.

About half the firms felt that partnership would catalyse conflict rather than harmony. Partnership would require an outward looking co-operative approach with the emphasis firmly on investment benefits rather than the pre-occupation with expense. The sample firms were not at this stage of development. They were just not ready for partnership.

It can be persuasively argued that the key to a successful business resides in a sound marketing philosophy. Marketing does not exist in isolation. It may be regarded as a total integrating activity. Relevant consultancy could have assisted the south Wessex firms in this respect. The problem was that the firms were not really aware of the former, and were not interested in the latter.

Performance

Could the performances of small firms be forecasted and measured? During the course of the South Wessex Survey an effort was made to indentify characteristics that might act as predictors of performance. It was hypothesised that successful companies (with an average annual rate of return of over 15% over the past five years) might possess certain attributes that stood them apart from less successful firms (those with less than 15% return on capital). The two groups were compared using a wide range of attributes.

It appeared that the more successful firms placed, for example, less importance on consolidation and more on long term growth. They were less likely to use committees to make decisions. The overall impression was that the successful companies were more likely to be market oriented, offer a small range of products, have a leaner staff and operate a more intensive appraisal of capital projects. They were also more likely to have newer, more productive and higher quality plant and equipment.

The findings provided some evidence that successful firms could be distinguished from less successful companies, and suggested strongly that a small number of managerial factors could possibly predict financial performance. In the main, the attributes indicated that the progressive firms were highlighted by objectives that focussed on positive aspects such as exporting, market research, etc., rather than upon negative issues such as conserving at all costs the present situation in order to simply survive.

Some small businesses have virtually no organisational blueprint, no managerial structure or financial discipline. The small hotel turned out to be a case in point. It defied the collection of data for the building of a forecasting corporate performance model. Intended initially as a

156

contrast to the small engineering firm 10 year study, the small hotel sub-survey tended to reinforce the findings of the South Wessex Survey. The sub-survey covered the period 1986-1991 and was undertaken in 30 small hotels. It revealed serious problems of investment and related sub-optimality across the spectrum.

Most of the hotels had persisted with their own methods of operation over the years and, again, the flexibility that might be expected from the small hotel was not apparent. Current demand was the fundamental determinant of business. Management initiatives to attract business, especially in the off peak season, took second place to this.

The principal goal of about one quarter of the hotels was reasonable profit, but 'remaining in business' was a strong underpinning component. As with the small engineering firm, many of the hotels regarded survival as evidence of success.

Owner-manager turnover was far more rapid than for the small firm. Just under 50% had been in the hotel business for fewer than six years. Hardly any owners had formal qualifications in the hotel and catering trades. Some owners even had outside jobs themselves. Attitudes towards staff training were rather poor.

Prices charged tended to be below what the market might have been expected to bear. Local rivalry was the major determinant of price and not the facilities on offer. Financial performance was patently adversely affected by this. As for investment, general refurbishing was the main priority. Marketing policies by a massive 90% of the sample were virtually nil.

Current value added tax posed a problem. Some 60% of the sample hotels had not considered it worthwhile exceeding the VAT limit and had not registered.

The hotels' aims were 'family orientated' rather than 'business' and as such the hotels under scrutiny created a high risk environment for themselves.

As with the small engineering firm the small hotel owner exhibited similar managerial weaknesses eminating essentially from background and, not least, family attitudes to business. Each hotel possessed its own idiosyncratic philosophy of operation that made it virtually impossible to extract data for a model comprising attributes for the forecasting of performance.

A similar problem where characteristics could not easily be collected for performance forecasting concerned staffing in the South Wessex Survey firms. This came as a surprise. It was expected that here was an area that might lend itself for performance measurement.

Most of the south Wessex firms had problems regarding the number of people to employ for optimum operation. Errors in staffing were readily observable. The necessity criterion, once again, was the substitute for the productive employment of staff. There were even instances of seasonal misjudgement by the firms in that they had not estimated correctly the costs of not engaging the optimum number of staff. There was also, of course, a serious training problem inherent in this.

There were occasions where staff teams were not at full capacity. Some staff were dissatisfied with the jobs they were doing and there were no obvious remedies offered by management. Inadequate delegation by management seemed to be a common feature of the total system.

The subjective nature of these examples rendered them virtually incapable of incorporation into models to guide management towards improving performance. More than this, the unpredictable nature of the variables made the measuring of staff performance difficult, and especially since staff were not always consulted when measurement was contemplated. This posed a serious problem where management had set pay levels on such measurement. Salary miscalculations could be expensive for management and a few south Wessex firms had experienced the repercussions. Strangely, the influence of the trades unions had not enjoyed much prominence in these decisions. All this was somewhat surprising since on the general subject of staff motivation the major response by over three quarters of the sample firms was that of pay.

Finally, however small the south Wessex firm was it, nevertheless, comprised an extremely complicated business unit. The Wessex investigation showed that models to predict business performance were patently more applicable in some areas than others, not least as a result of the human variables falling into the categories of the immeasurable and the unpredictable.

Finalities

The South Wessex Survey findings have strongly suggested that the firms' business behaviour and managerial decision making were persistently inconsistent with any reasonable yardstick of optimality. The small firms under review appeared to ignore, and even avoid, opportunities for improved performances, financial or otherwise, across the board. The endemic problems encountered and the pre-occupation with survival were particularly evident in the very small firms and in the mechanical engineering as opposed to the electrical engineering firms. Almost inevitably as a consequence of these non-rigorous approaches, returns on capital were likely to remain below those levels reasonably attainable. Despite any limitations of the sample, data collection procedures over the ten year period, data analysis, consultancy applications and research interpretation, the overall picture cannot be simply disregared.

The consultant can make recommendations but will the small firm adopt them? Small firms do not employ consultants as a rule, and even if they do the chances of the firms actually implementing recommendations are remote. For example, during the course of consultancies undertaken, taxation and related matters are often raised. As a first step towards an exploration of the tax situation an elementary abridged guide to taxation for the smaller firm often proved helpful as a catalyst for discussion. Some of the tax problems encountered included:

Tax planning
Taxable profits
Trading losses
Capital allowances
Capital gains tax
Corporation tax
Tax payments
Close companies
Value added tax
Enforcement powers of the Revenue
Tax effective finance
Raising share capital
Tax effective remuneration packages
Employing members of the family
Children at work
Executive benefits
Company cars
Medical cover
Share incentive schemes
Profit related pay
Dividend policy
Pension planning
Selling shareholdings
Purchasing own shares
Property for directors' use
Inheritance tax

In some instances an expert tax consultant was suggested but few firms acknowledged this need. They opted, in the main, to rely on the hope that the tax problem was not serious. A tax consultant would be considered to be unnecessary, and especially at the rates charged. There was usually a preference to stumble through the tax maze rather than engage an expert to guide them through it. This attitude was, of course, widely prevalent in other facets of small business management.

The root of the problem could lie within a communicational, if not educational impasse. The universities and polytechnics with their short courses, degrees and post-graduate work, together with the professional bodies' courses could, on the face of it, provide the framework for far more opportunities for the small firm manager to confront and attack the problems. The C.B.I., the Institute of Directors, Local Authorities, the Engineering Associations and consultancy facilities could, and should, look again at more positive ways of persuading small firms to seek advice as a routine rather than when it is usually too late.

Small firms react favourably to the personal face to face contact with the local consultant who is on hand over the longer term, who knows the firm well, who charges reasonable fees on a payment by results basis and is well known to the firm. But above all the firms themselves must start to appraise and monitor their own performances, preferably under guidance, far more purposefully than they appear to be doing. The importance of this guidance, and effective training generally, cannot be over emphasised for the smaller firm during the 1990's and onwards into the twenty first century.